AGING INTO THE 21st CENTURY

Aging Into the 21st Century

MIDDLE-AGERS TODAY

Edited by
[*LISSY F. JARVIK, M.D., Ph.D.*]

VETERANS ADMINISTRATION (BRENTWOOD) and

UNIVERSITY OF CALIFORNIA, LOS ANGELES

HELENE KRATZ, Assistant Editor

GARDNER PRESS, INC., NEW YORK
Distributed by HALSTED PRESS
Division of John Wiley & Sons, Inc.

New York • Toronto • London • Sydney

Grateful acknowledgment is made to Pamela A. Schaff for valuable assistance in preparing the manuscript for publication.

Views Expressed—These chapters are the authors' and are not to be attributed to the editor unless expressly so stated.

GARDNER PRESS, INC.
19 Union Square West
New York 10003

Distributed solely by the Halsted Press Division
of John Wiley & Sons, Inc., New York

Library of Congress Cataloging in Publication Data
Main entry under title:

Aging into the 21st century.

Includes index.
1. Old age—Addresses, essays, lectures.
2. Aging—Addresses, essays, lectures. 3. Aged—Psychology—Addresses, essays, lectures. I. Jarvik, Lissy F. II. Kratz, Helene.
HQ1061.A47   301.43'5   77-25837
ISBN 0-470-99370-7

Printed in the United States of America

This book is dedicated to Gordon Tomkins,
one of the contributors to this volume,
whose chance to age into the 21st century
terminated at the age of 49
while this manuscript was awaiting pre-publication revision.
Humanist, musician, physician, scholar, scientist, visionary
—and friend,
—he is deeply missed.

Contents

PART TWO
SOCIETAL RESPONSE:
PSYCHOLOGICAL PERSPECTIVES

CONTRIBUTORS

Roslyn B. Alfin-Slater, Ph.D., Professor and Division Head, Environmental and Nutritional Sciences, School of Public Health, University of California, Los Angeles, California.

James E. Birren, Ph.D., Executive Director, Ethel Percy Andrus Gerontology Center, Dean, Leonard Davis School of Gerontology, University of Southern California, Los Angeles, California.

Alexander Comfort, M.B., B.Ch., M.A., Cantab; Ph.D., D.Sc., Lond., Institute for Higher Studies, McGuire House, Santa Barbara, California, Clinical Lecturer in Psychiatry, Stanford University, Professor, Department Pathology, University of California, Irvine.

Christian de Duve, M.D., Andrew W. Mellon Professor, The Rockefeller University, New York, New York, President, International Institute of Cellular and Molecular Pathology, Brussels, Belgium.

Carl Eisdorfer, M.D., Ph.D., Professor and Chairman, Psychiatry and Behavioral Sciences, University of Washington, Seattle, Washington.

Marjorie Fiske, Ph.D., Professor and Director, Human Development Program, University of California, San Francisco, California.

Ruth Friedman, B.A., School of Public Health, University of California, Los Angeles, California.

Martin Grotjahn, M.D., Rothchild Professor, University of Southern California, Los Angeles, California, Clinical Professor Emeritus, University of Southern California, Los Angeles, California, Training Analyst, Southern California Psychoanalytic Institute.

Lissy F. Jarvik, M.D., Ph.D., Professor, Department of Psychiatry, University of California, Los Angeles, California, and

Chief, Psychogenetic Unit, Veterans Administration Hospital (Brentwood), Los Angeles, California.

Asenath A. La Rue, Ph.D., Lecturer in Psychology, California State College, Dominguez Hills, and Staff Research Associate, Department of Psychiatry, University of California, Los Angeles, California, and Consultant, Psychogenetics Unit, Veterans Administration Hospital (Brentwood), Los Angeles, California.

Roslyn Lindheim, Ph.D., Professor of Architecture, College of Environmental Design, University of California, Berkeley, California.

George L. Maddox, Ph.D., Director, Center for the Study of Aging and Human Development, Duke University Medical Center, Durham, North Carolina.

Howard Y. McClusky, Ph.D., Professor of Education, School of Education, Faculty Associate, Institute of Gerontology, University of Michigan, Ann Arbor, Michigan.

David D. McFarland, Ph.D., Associate Professor, Department of Sociology, University of California, Los Angeles, California.

Bernice L. Neugarten, Ph.D., Professor, Committee on Human Development, Department of Behavioral Sciences, University of Chicago, Chicago, Illinois.

Gordon M. Tomkins, M.D., Ph.D., Professor of Biochemistry and Vice-Chairman, Department of Biochemistry and Biophysics, University of California, San Francisco, California.

INTRODUCTION

Grow old along with me!
The best is yet to be
The last of life for which the first was made.

Was it but yesterday when Robert Browning's familiar words struck a note of belief in the hearts of many —arousing a vision of the future as a time of retirement, of easy life, of freedom from the worries, the cares and the pressures of earlier years? When Social Security was a siren's call, promising freedom from the fear of poverty? And when medical discoveries, increasing at a geometric rate, seemed to offer freedom from the fear of pain and illness? Today, as we look at the isolation, the loneliness, the financial hardships and the many other indignities of old age, we begin to wonder about the marvels of a technology which promises longer life and easier ways of doing almost everything—except growing old. As we go into the 21st century, there will be increasingly large numbers of those considered "aged." All those born in 1936 or before will be included in that group, if we define as "aged" anyone 65 years and older. And, 30 million of us are expected to survive into the 21st century (assuming a slight decrease in mortality rates). Are we going to encounter the same appallingly high rate of physical and mental illness that exists among the aged of today? What, if anything, is now being done to reduce this high morbidity? What is being done to help the elderly cope with mounting physical and psychosocial stresses which are their lot? What, if anything, is now being done to help them meet their own needs? What ought to be done? Surely, we need a reversal of the current trend whereby the elderly seem to consume more and more while contributing less and less to the Gross National Product and to society as a whole. It appears that as of now all forces are conspiring to increase the uselessness of the old and at the same time to decrease their social standing in accord with lowered usefulness. We cut them off from the resources they need for maintaining themselves in any semblance of self-sufficiency and then penalize them for their reduced productivity. Should this trend continue, it is bound to lead to personal destruction and pain and sorrow on a level never before experienced by so many of our citizens. And their number may become legion, if we take, for example, Gordon Tomkins' suggestion that by altering cellular communication we may succeed in extending the lifespan so far as to bring the achievement of some measure of immortality within the realm of possibility. It is not likely to happen in our lifetime, and, unfortunately, Gordon Tomkins' own life has already been cut short. Yet, we need to think about the consequences of a marked prolongation in lifespan. How would it affect the daily activities of people? Their outlook on life? Their interactions? What would happen to our resources, natural and artificial? To the labor market? There are myriad questions and very few answers.

Christian de Duve, 1976 Nobel Prize winner, hopes that the world of the future will be a nurturing place for what we do know and what we can achieve. Neither de Duve nor Tomkins has been identified with pronouncements regarding immortality or rejuvenation. Both have, in fact, been involved with work that is at the very basis of life—intracellular mechanisms. Nonetheless, both have posed possible paths for changing human life as we now know it. Other contributors, too, have addressed themselves to future issues as they can be anticipated from present day knowledge, be it in applied biology (where Alex Comfort serves us a flavorful cocktail of fact richly spiced with fancy), in applied psychology (where Martin Grotjahn leads us into the world of group therapy), or in applied sociology (where George Maddox robs us of the illusion of a future gerontocracy). Pessimism, like that seen in David McFarland's demographic speculations, in Carl Eisdorfer's frightening example of futuristic death houses, or in Marjorie Fiske's poignant projection of male and female life trajectories on a collision course, is found side by side with guarded optimism as expressed in Bernice Neugarten's expectation of an "age-irrelevant" society, or in Asenath LaRue's and Lissy Jarvik's hope that for many of the aged in the 21st century intellectual decline may become but a myth. All is counterbalanced by unbounded enthusiasm as depicted by Roslyn Alfin-Slater's belief in a possible revolution in nutritional habits, Roslyn Lindheim's architectural designs for future living, and Howard McClusky's vibrant advocacy of widely varying designs for an educational future where lifelong learning will be a sine qua non.

In their own styles and with their own highly individualized approaches, the authors have spoken out defining problems, describing attitudes, decrying limits, occasionally giving answers, and frequently speaking with the voices of prophecy. In the period during which this book was being compiled, some of these prophecies have already been fulfilled: area legislation has been enacted; a National Institute on Aging has been created within the National Institutes of Health, and its Director, Dr. Robert N. Butler, has begun energetically to pursue the goal of advancing research in the interest of the aged. Some of it is already in progress; some of it is new and innovative in the field of gerontology—a very young discipline.

A remarkable change in attitude is taking place throughout the land. It is hoped that this volume will be one more catalyst to help accelerate and perpetuate the trend toward accepting the aged as a large, heterogeneous group of people with differing tastes and needs, whose ability to savor life may change, but not necessarily diminish, with the passage of time.

1

THE AGED IN THE 21st CENTURY:
A Demographer's View

DAVID D. McFARLAND

At the time of the 1970 United States Census, persons over 65 years of age numbered 20 million and constituted just slightly less than 10% of the United States population.

However, both popular news media and scientific journals have recently published articles containing predictions of remarkable increases in the numbers and proportions of elderly persons over the course of the next several decades. In Time magazine it was recently stated that ". . . 20% of the American population will be over 65 by the year 2000 . . ."; the article then went on to use that prediction as the justification for a further prediction, of "oldsters developing into a formidable pressure group demanding more sympathetic treatment from society" ("The Joy of Aging," 1976). Constance Holden, writing in Science, went 5% further, asserting that "People over 65 . . . will . . . by the year 2000 constitute an unprecedented

25 percent of the population" (Holden, 1976; see, however, Myers, 1976).

In fact, neither *Time*'s 20% nor Holden's 25% is at all plausible, given the current age composition of the United States population and the short amount of time between now and the year 2000. By the year 2000 the absolute *number* of persons 65 or older will increase substantially, from 20 million to approximately 30 million, but the entire population will also increase substantially, from slightly over 200 million to somewhere approaching 300 million; therefore, the proportion of persons 65 and older will remain in the vicinity of 10%—perhaps 8%, or possibly 12%, but certainly neither 20% nor 25%.

If the elderly in the year 2000 constitute "a formidable pressure group" to a greater extent than they do today, it will be because they have substantially improved their political organization and mobilization and not because of any substantial increase in their numbers relative to the numbers in other age groups.

What, precisely, is the basis for calling one prediction "plausible" and another "implausible"? Just what can we know, and with what degree of certainty, about the short-term future and about the more remote future? These are the kinds of issues to which the remainder of this chapter is devoted, considering in each case predictions regarding the elderly in the 21st century.

There is at least one surprise in store for readers who have not been trained in formal demography: increased longevity does not necessarily imply increasing proportions of elderly; the age composition of a population depends primarily on the levels of fertility it has experienced and not, as one may intuitively think, on the levels of mortality it has experienced. Near the end of the chapter we will indicate why this is so, and also will spell out its implications for those of us who are concerned with forecasting the future of the elderly component of the population.

Discussions of the future tend to stimulate flights of fantasy. However, two aspects of the present topic should tend to promote caution: (1) the 21st century is, after all, only a few years hence and (2) demographic changes, except those concerning fertility, occur much more slowly than many other kinds of changes.

In considering the 21st century, the first thing to notice is how close it is to the present. Students who will graduate from college in the year 2000 will have their births tallied as this book goes to press. Scholars who will receive PhD's and take faculty positions in the year 2000 are already on the scene, typically attending kindergarten. The 65-year-olds who will retire in the year 2000 are already age 42. Furthermore, and more directly relevant to the question of the elderly becoming "a formidable pressure group," nearly everyone who will be old enough to vote in the year 2000 is already alive.

The closeness of the 21st century is extremely important, in that it categorically precludes changes of certain kinds during the interim. Genetic mutations may eventually lead to the evolution of a longer-lived species, and the United States in the year 3000 may contain a much higher proportion of elderly than present. However, the genetic composition of the population in the year 2000 could not possibly differ too much from that of the current population since most of the people who will be alive in 2000 are already alive today and already have their genetic structures determined.

A second important consideration is the relatively slow pace of demographic change, compared to many other kinds of change. A human produces relatively few offspring and does so only after a considerable delay in time. Human babies are produced one at a time, not in litters as with some species of animals; and biological maturation in combination with lengthy socialization into adult roles results in an average age at childbearing in excess of 25 years, in contrast with that of many animals, which reproduce themselves within as little as one year.

Many kinds of changes have no such restrictions. An innovation in technology may expand in a matter of months from a handful of experimental units to widespread mass-produced copies. Consider the recent "explosion" in the ownership of pocket-sized electronic calculators. Or consider the "explosion" in the use of contraceptive pills which occurred a few years ago.

The rapidity of growth processes is sometimes expressed in terms of doubling times—the length of time required for the items being considered to double in number. Although demographers sometimes talk about "the population explosion," they are in fact dealing with a growth process whose doubling time is measured in decades, not in months or years as are the doubling times for the numbers of users of various technological innovations, and certainly not in fractions of seconds as are the doubling times for the number of atomic particles involved in literal explosions.

Mortality conditions, too, change relatively slowly, so

there is good reason to anticipate that this will continue to be the case, and hence that mortality conditions in the near future will resemble those of the recent past. Changes in fertility are more pronounced and less predictable, but that fact has little importance for many purposes: the numbers of elderly can be forecast as far into the future as the 2030s without making any assumptions about future fertility levels since anyone who will be elderly between now and then is already alive now.

Population Projections and Population Forecasts

Demographers often insist, with what is really undue modesty, that their professional skills enable them to provide only "projections," not "forecasts." To make a projection is merely to work out the logical implications of a set of assumptions which may or may not be true. To make a forecast, in contrast, is to predict what is really to happen in the future (see Keyfitz, 1972).

In practice, the distinction is sometimes muddled by authors who, although certainly involved in attempts to predict future happenings, call their works "projections" instead of "forecasts," presumably to enable them to deny responsibility for whatever discrepancies are later found between the future they have foreseen and the future that actually has arrived. Indeed, the United States Census Bureau follows this practice.

Both projections and forecasts ordinarily involve assertions about events in a later time period, deduced from observed events in an earlier time period, together with assumptions about the nature of change during the interim. The distinction resides in the nature of the claims the demographer is making. A "forecast" is an unconditional assertion which the demographer presents as the best guess about the truth; a "projection," in contrast, is a conditional assertion which, aside from the possibility of computational error, is tautologically true.

"The number of 65-year-olds in the United States in the year 2000 will be approximately 1.68 million" would constitute a forecast. It is unconditional, in the sense that it contains no loopholes. Its truth or falsehood is not known at present, but when the 2000 census results become available its accuracy can then be determined.

"If death rates were to remain at current levels, and if net migration were to be negligible, then the number of 65-year-olds in the United States in 2000 would be approximately 1.68 million"—this statement would constitute a projection. It is a conditional assertion and, except for the possibility of arithmetical error, is tautologically true. Should the census figures for the year 2000 subsequently be found to differ markedly from 1.68 million, that would indicate not that the assertion had been in error but only that its assumptions had not been met—that death rates had not remained at current levels, or that net migration had not been negligible.

In making a forecast, one uses assumptions one believes to be true, or at least assumptions one regards as reasonable guesses about the truth. However, in making a projection, one will sometimes deliberately use assumptions one believes to be untrue. "If death rates from major cardiovascular diseases were to drop to zero as of 1970, if death rates from all other causes were to remain at their current levels, and if net migration were to be negligible, the number of 65-year-olds in the United States in the year 2000 would be approximately 1.91 million"—this assertion would constitute another projection. It is equally valid as a projection, since it too, except for the possibility of arithmetical error, is tautologically true. Yet one would hardly forecast 1.91 million 65-year-olds in 2000. This author, at least, believes the assumption of elimination of deaths from heart disease to be not only false but nowhere near the truth about what will happen to death rates between 1970 and 2000. Census Bureau demographers agree (United States Bureau of the Census, 1973, p. 24).

Yet it may be a useful exercise to make projections based on assumptions one believes to be false. For one thing, it is often easier to specify assumptions one believes to be false than to specify assumptions one believes to be true. This author does not anticipate, for example, that death rates will remain at their current levels—some improvement seems likely. On the other hand, this author does anticipate that the improvement will be nowhere nearly as substantial as that brought about by a cure of major cardiovascular disease. Although it would be quite difficult for the present author to specify his best guess about the future, these two alternative assumptions—one with implausibly high mortality, the other with implausibly low mortality—provide limits between which he believes the truth almost certainly lies.

Population projections based on dubious or counter-factual assumptions have other legitimate uses unrelated to attempts to anticipate the future, but they need not concern us here. Next we shall turn to actual numerical results of calculations aimed at forecasting the elderly population to the year 2000 and beyond.

Numbers of Elderly in the 21st Century

Earlier in this chapter, we used arguments in which the temporal proximity of the year 2000 played a central part: The age distribution in the year 2000 will not differ dramatically from the current age distribution, we argued, because there simply is not sufficient time between now and then for any dramatic changes in the upper end of the age distribution to take place. Clearly, however, that type of argument breaks down when one turns from the year 2000 to the more remote future.

The United States Bureau of the Census (1973, 1976) has produced preliminary and revised reports on demographic aspects of the elderly, with which any serious student of this topic should become familiar. These rich sources of information provide, along with much additional material, figures for the numbers of elderly in the United States for selected future dates (United States Bureau of the Census, 1976, Table 2-1), as shown in Table 1.

It is established Census Bureau practice (which is in marked contrast to established Weather Bureau practice!) to call their figures "projections" rather than "forecasts." Yet it is quite clear that these figures are not just the implications of an arbitrarily selected set of assumptions but are indeed the results of serious attempts to predict what will

Table 1
Census Bureau Projections for the Number of Elderly in Selected Future Years:
Population (millions) in age group

| Year | Age group | | |
	55 years and above	65 years and above	75 years and above
1970	38.7	20.1	7.6
1980	45.6	24.5	9.1
1990	49.4	28.9	11.4
2000	53.5	30.6	13.5
2010	65.7	33.2	13.9
2020	79.5	42.8	15.4
2030	82.5	51.6	20.7
2040	84.8	50.3	24.2

really happen in the future. For one thing, the Census Bureau has revised certain figures (from the analogous figures in 1973, Table 1) as the dates in question have come closer and as additional relevant information has become available—a procedure hardly called for if mere projection as opposed to forecasting were involved. For another thing, the Census Bureau authors themselves treat these figures as forecasts at the point where they discuss the prospects of their predictions being accurate: "The projected numbers of elderly persons cited here should be close to the mark because they are unaffected by future fertility" (United States Bureau of the Census, 1976, p. 5). We will, therefore, as will undoubtedly the vast majority of other users, disregard the Census Bureau's labeling these figures as projections and we will regard them as forecasts.

The Census Bureau (1976) made its calculations assuming slightly declining mortality. It is also instructive, however, to make a baseline projection assuming no improvement in mortality conditions. The result would not be a plausible forecast: it seems too pessimistic. Yet it can be useful in helping to set limits within plausible forecasts must lie. Such a projection has been carried out, with the results shown in Table 2:

Table 2

Projected Number of Elderly Assuming Persistence of Current Vital Rates: Population (millions) in age group

	Age group [a]			
Year	55 Years and above	65 Years and above	75 Years and above	Total (all ages)
1970	38.7	20.1	7.6	203.2
1980	43.9	23.3	9.0	224.0*
1990	45.7	26.3	10.4	246.2*
2000	47.1	26.5	11.7	266.7*
2010	56.0	27.2	11.3	290.2*
2020	66.6	34.0	11.8	313.6*
2030	69.9*	40.5	15.8	337.1*
2040	75.9*	40.5*	18.1	360.8*
2050	79.6*	44.2*	17.3*	386.4*

[a] Figures marked with asterisks are affected by assumptions regarding future fertility.

These figures were excerpted from a projection which began with the 1970 census population figures and projected them forward in time, assuming constant fertility and mortality conditions. As indicated previously, this is an implausibly pessimistic assumption regarding mortality, so these numbers should be underpredictions of the numbers alive in the various age groups in the various years.

The fertility assumption, like the mortality assumption, is undoubtedly in error. However, one cannot assert with any reasonable degree of assurance whether actual fertility will be lower or higher than the level assumed. Therefore, the assumed level of fertility is neither implausibly high nor implausibly low; not even the direction, let alone the magnitude, of change in fertility levels can be predicted with any degree of certainty.

Fortunately, however, most of these projected population figures (all except those marked with asterisks) are completely unaffected by whatever assumptions are made regarding fertility. For example, everyone who will be age 65 or over in 2030 already has been born by 1970, the year in which census figures form the initial population for these projections, and hence their numbers in 2030 depend only on their numbers in 1970 and subsequent mortality conditions, and not on subsequent fertility conditions.

According to calculations not shown here, and still assuming constant vital rates, the annual number of persons reaching age 65 increases from some 1.5 million in 1970 to a peak of approximately 1.9 million in the latter 1980s and thereafter declines to approximately 1.7 million by the year 2000.

The total numbers age 65 and older behave similarly but with a lag of nearly a decade, increasing from approximately 20.1 million in 1970 to a peak of approximately 26.9 million in 1995 and thereafter declining somewhat to approximately 26.5 million by the year 2000. When mortality is held constant, as in this projection, low fertility during the depression of the 1930s is reflected in reduced numbers entering retirement during the 1990s.

The same kinds of projections may be made farther into the future, using data on numbers of births in more recent years. With mortality held constant, the number entering the 65 and older age group each year is proportional to the number of births 65 years earlier. However, the numbers of annual births increased systematically from some 2 million around 1930 to approximately 4¼ million per year in 1957–1960, thereafter dropping precipitously, although somewhat irregularly, to about 3 million in the most recent birth cohorts. The increase from

1945 to 1947 was particularly steep and is often referred to as the beginning of a "baby boom" following World War II.

The corresponding projections, assuming constant mortality, give the following high points: The numbers turning 65 each year will increase until about 2025 (when the 1960 birth cohort will become age 65) and will then begin a sharp decline lasting over a decade. The rise in numbers turning 65 will be steepest about 2011 (when the 1946 birth cohort will become age 65). The total numbers age 65 and older will fluctuate similarly, but less markedly, and with a lag of nearly a decade.

This type of analysis will carry us through the years until about 2040, when persons not yet born at the time our projections began will begin to reach retirement age. For the more remote future we need a different kind of analysis, to which we shall turn in a later section.

Each of these figures, it should be remembered, is one the present author believes to be false. The actual numbers are expected to be higher than these projections, because these projections have assumed constant mortality conditions when, in fact, the present author expects mortality conditions will improve somewhat.

Next, let us consider alternative projections, also believed to be false but believed to err in the opposite direction. These alternative projections, assuming implausibly great reductions in mortality, would be expected to overpredict the numbers of elderly in the future. One such projection we have carried out assumes that the death rate applicable to any particular age group is 2% less than that applicable to the same age group during the previous year.

The results may be compared with those of the projection
assuming 1% annual reduction in mortality rates, the projection assuming no reduction in mortality rates, and the
Census Bureau projections assuming "slightly" or "rapidly" declining mortality. For the year 2000 these various
projections give the figures shown in Table 3.

Table 3
Alternative Projections of Elderly Population for Year 2000:
Population (millions) in age group

| | Age group | | | |
Projection	55 years and above	65 years and above	75 years and above	Total
Current rates	47.1	26.5	11.7	266.7
Census Bureau 1%/year	53.5	30.6	13.5	—
mortality reduction	52.2	30.9	14.8	273.6
Census Bureau "rapid" mortality reduction	—	32.6	—	—
2%/year mortality reduction	57.2	35.3	18.1	280.1

From these results it appears that various alternatives
among plausible sets of assumptions yield rather similar
conclusions about the numbers of elderly in the year 2000.
It is the case, however, that the alternative projections become more and more divergent as they go farther into the
future.

Projections Distinguishing Causes of Death

One may make projections in which the probability of a
person's dying during the next year, given that he or she

has attained a specified age, is broken down into several different probabilities of deaths attributed primarily to several different causes. The projected population remains unchanged; the only difference is that this projection keeps track of causes of deaths.

However, one may take the next step, once different causes of death are distinguished, to make projections assuming that the age-specific probabilities for dying from some cause has been reduced, whereas those for other causes have remained at their current values. One answers, then, the hypothetical question: What would the projected population be if medical advances reduced the probability of death from one cause but left other causes unchanged?

The effects, quite generally, are smaller than may be expected. A quite remarkable medical advance in the treatment of one disease may have only a slight effect on the resulting population. The reason is simple, once it is pointed out: A reduction in deaths from one disease implies an increase in the subsequent numbers at risk of deaths from that and other diseases, and hence an increase in the subsequent numbers of deaths from other diseases. If heart disease doesn't get you, cancer will.

This point may be illustrated by the results of selected projections making alternative assumptions about reductions in age- and cause-specific death rates. For these projections, current cause-specific death rates were aggregated into three groups: heart diseases, cancer, and all other causes. The projected numbers age 65 and 75 in the year 2000 have been calculated (Table 4) alternatively assuming that the age- and cause-specific death rates either

Table 4
Effects of Alternative Assumptions about Mortality Conditions

Projection	Number age 65	Number age 75
Current rates	1.681 million	1.284 million
Cancer reduced 10%	1.692	1.302
Heart disease reduced 10%	1.703	1.331
Cancer reduced 100%	1.799	1.482
Heart disease reduced 100%	1.912	1.834
Both reduced 100%	2.045	2.112

remain at current levels, or are reduced in 1970 by 10% and remain at those new levels, or are completely eliminated as of 1970.

The latter three projections, assuming complete elimination of deaths from heart disease and/or cancer, are regarded as highly implausible. The main conclusion here, then, is that the more plausible assumptions yield fairly small differences in the predicted numbers surviving at various ages.

The Age Distribution in the Remote Future

Vital rates fluctuate from year to year, and the age distribution fluctuates in a parallel but lagging manner. Nevertheless, a particular set of vital rates may be illuminated by asking what are the implications of those particular rates persisting a long time into the future. This is so because, with the persistence of fixed vital rates, the age distribution of the population eventually loses the irregular shape which reflects previous fluctuations in vital rates and takes on a shape which persists thereafter and which depends solely on the hypothetically unchanging set of vital rates (see, e.g., McFarland, 1969). This population projection yields useful information even if it does not qualify as a forecast, and even if one does not believe that the specified vital rates will, in fact, remain constant into the future.

The stable age distribution, which would eventually result from fixed age-specific vital rates, would have an age distribution given by:

$$c(a) = be^{-ra}p(a); \tag{1}$$

where $c(a)$ is the proportion in an increment of ages from a to $a + da$, b and r are the rates of birth and of natural increase, respectively, and $p(a)$ is the probability of survival from birth to age a. Therefore, the relative numbers of persons of two different ages, say a and a', are:

$$c(a)/c(a') = e^{-r(a-a')}p(a)/p(a'). \tag{2}$$

The exponential factor involving the growth rate r arises from the different sizes of the two cohorts at birth; in a population whose rate of growth is only modestly different from zero, cohorts born several decades apart will still differ substantially in cohort size at birth.

Consider, for example, the relative numbers of 80-year-olds and 40-year-olds. The factor $p(80)/p(40)$ is already nearly 0.3 in the United States and by definition cannot exceed unity, so the factor $p(80)/p(40)$ must vary by less than 400%, no matter how dramatic the improvements in mortality reduction. Turn next to the factor $e^{-r(a-a')}$, which covers the relative size at birth of the two cohorts born $a - a' = 40$ years apart. Fertility is sufficiently unpredictable that neither 5% annual increase nor 5% annual decrease of the population is implausibly extreme. These annual differences, although seemingly slight, compound as dramatically as the interest due on a revolving charge account. If one may suppose annual increase to be anywhere between $+.05$ and $-.05$, then the factor covering the relative size at birth of two cohorts born 40 years apart may be anywhere between $e^{-(.05)\ (40)} = .14$ and $e^{-(-.05)\ (40)} = 7.4$, the larger of which is some 5000% of the smaller.

If, however, as in the United States, mortality prior to completion of childbearing is negligible, the value of r depends almost entirely on fertility and only negligibly on mortality. The growth rate r is the solution of the equation:

$$\int_0^\beta e^{-ra} m(a)\, da = 1, \tag{3}$$

where β is the highest age of childbearing and $m(a)$ is the age-specific proportion of women bearing female children. [In general, the integrand would include the factor $p(a)$, the probability of survival to age a, but in the United States that factor is essentially unity for ages below β.]

The relative number of 80- and 40-year-olds in the more remote future is, therefore, confined within 400% as far as variability caused by improved mortality conditions is concerned, but it can easily vary 5000% because of the unpredictability of future fertility. The age distribution in the remote future therefore depends little on future changes in mortality and depends primarily on future business cycles, fads in life style, and whatever other poorly understood factors affect fertility.

References

Holden, C. National Institute on Aging: New focus on growing old. *Science,* 1976, *193,* 1081.

Keyfitz, N. On future population. *Journal of the American Statistical Association,* 1972, *67,* 347–363.

McFarland, D. D. On the theory of stable populations: A new and elementary proof of the theorems under weaker assumptions. *Demography,* 1969, *6,* 301–322.

Myers, G. C. Demographic data on the elderly. *Science,* 1976, *193,*358.

The joy of aging. *Time,* November 8, 1976, p. 86.

United States Bureau of the Census. Some demographic aspects of aging in the United States. *Current Population Reports,* Series P-23, No. 59. Washington, D. C.: United States Government Printing Office, 1973.

United States Bureau of the Census. Demographic aspects of aging and the older population in the United States. *Current Population Reports,* Series P-23. No. 59. Washington, D. C.: United States Government Printing Office, 1976.

Some of the research upon which this paper is based was performed pursuant to Contract No. NIH-NICHD-72-2766 with the National Institutes of Health, Department of Health, Education and Welfare, David D. McFarland, Principal Investigator. Additional financial support was received from Grant No. NSF-G1-39091 from the National Science Foundation, Bernice L. Neugarten, Principal Investigator.

PART ONE
IS THE LIFE-SPAN EXPANDABLE?
Biological Perspectives
COMMENTARY

McFarland has set the stage by providing projections and forecasts, as he carefully differentiates them, on what numbers of individuals in various age groups will be present in the United States as we go into the 21st century. He has made a persuasive argument against a drastic reduction in age-specific mortality rates by the year 2000—even if deaths due to cardiovascular diseases and cancer were to be eliminated. He cautions, therefore, against expecting a marked increase in the *proportion* of aged individuals at the beginning of the 21st century. Yet, eliminating deaths from cardiovascular disease alone would increase the 75-year-olds by 43% above projections based on current rates (Table 4). All those who will be over age 65 by the year 2000 were born some time ago, before 1935 to be exact, and we can calculate the expected *number* of survivors with a fairly high probability of being correct. Their *proportion* in the population, however, is a function of the birth rate during the remainder of the 20th century, and predicting that is fraught with uncertainties. Nonetheless, some of the contributors to this volume have remained undeterred and have moved on to speculation. However, we must live with McFarland's figures while we await the outcome of changes in customs and the results of critical experiments altering the rate of aging. Such experiments will undoubtedly be performed in the coming decades, inspired largely by the work of imaginative scientists such as de Duve and Tomkins. We cannot predict the likelihood of "breakthroughs" occurring during the 21st century; at this point we can hear only the early-warning rumblings of new approaches to the multifaceted problems of aging. The paucity of information and experimentation in gerontology emphasizes our profound ignorance in this field. It underscores Alex Comfort's plea for more liberal support of research efforts and application of knowledge already available to insure a healthier and more satisfying old age. One way of doing so is elaborated in the concluding chapter of this section in which Roslyn Alfin-Slater and Ruth Friedman tackle one of the most neglected areas in health behavior—nutrition.

2

CELLS AGE:
Are Lysosomes Among The Villains?

CHRISTIAN de DUVE

The possible role of lysosomes in cellular senescence is best appreciated in relation to the role played by these particles in preventing cells from aging.

It is a well-known fact that most intracellular components are continuously renewed. In a long-lived cell, such as a neuron, this phenomenon of turnover brings about a constant rejuvenation of the cell contents. For instance, when we say that a nerve cell has the age of the individual to whom it belongs, we must keep in mind that most of the molecules that compose this cell are considerably younger. Many are less than a week old; some even turn over several times a day; and very few date back more than a few months. An old cell is very much like an old city. Whereas the town as a whole may go back many centuries, most of its buildings have been destroyed and reconstructed many times.

Turnover means not only synthesis of new molecules and structures, but also breakdown of preexisting ones. If the cell itself is to remain unchanged, the two processes must balance each other quantitatively and qualitatively. Much remains to be learned concerning the controlled breakdown of intracellular constituents, but there are good reasons to believe that lysosomes play a significant role in this process, perhaps even a major one.

It is known that lysosomes contain a complete digestive system capable of bringing about the extensive hydrolytic breakdown of all major cell constituents, including proteins, nucleic acids, carbohydrates, and lipids. No other comparable complement of enzymes has been detected elsewhere in the cell. Lysosomes thereby appear to be the only cell part so far identified as possessing the ability to accomplish the kind of generalized degradation required by turnover.

It is also known that lysosomes are normally involved in the segregation and digestion of mitochondria, membrane fragments, ribosomes, and other cell constituents. The detailed mechanism and quantitative importance of this process, which is called cellular autophagy, are not completely elucidated. But its existence and physiological significance have been clearly demonstrated.

There can be no doubt, therefore, that lysosomes participate significantly in the controlled breakdown of cellular constituents which underlies turnover and allows living cells to replace worn-out parts of their machinery by newly synthesized ones. Only the quantitative importance of the contribution of lysosomes to normal self-degradation is uncertain. Also unsettled is the specificity of autophagic segregation. We should like to think of this process as removing preferentially defective molecules and organelles, but there is no firm evidence that this is so.

Granting that the part played by lysosomes in turnover is more than trivial, it is clear that any deterioration, quantitative or qualitative, of their performance should affect adversely the cells concerned. Rejuvenation will be impaired, which is not very different from saying that aging will be promoted. In recent years, work by the Gershons (1973), Holliday and Tarrant (1972), and others has drawn attention to the accumulation of defective enzyme molecules in aging cells. These results have generally been interpreted as reflecting errors in protein synthesis, in agreement with the error catastrophy hypothesis of Orgel (1963). The alternative possibility, of an impairment in the autophagic removal of defective enzyme molecules, bears consideration.

Turning now to the lysosomes themselves, we may inquire how they are likely to be affected by the performance of their duties. Ideally, they should not be. They should emerge essentially unchanged from an autophagic event, provided the segregated material is digested completely and the products of that digestion are transferred quantitatively to the cytoplasm, by diffusion or otherwise. This is so most of the time, but occasionally molecules enter the lysosomes, or arise within them, that are both resistant to enzymatic digestion and unable to pass across the lysosomal membrane. This can happen not only in the course of autophagy, but also during heterophagy, the digestion in lysosomes of materials taken up from the outside by endocytosis. In cells lacking the ability to discharge the contents of their lysosomes into the outside medium by exocytosis or defecation, a deficiency common to many cell

types, there is no other possible fate for nonpermeant un-
degradable materials trapped inside lysosomes than to remain indefinitely within these particles. This is indeed
what is observed in aging cells throughout the animal
kingdom, from protozoa to the human brain. The material
most commonly found accumulating in lysosomes is
lipofuscin, the so-called "age pigment," a resin-like substance made up of protein and other molecules cross-
linked by bifunctional aldehydes, which themselves probably arise from lipid peroxidation.

All this is well documented. As cells grow older, their
lysosomes become progressively loaded with undigestible
residues and thereby occupy an increasing fraction of the
cytoplasmic volume. Thus, unlike most other cellular constituents, which are continuously renewed, lysosomes may
be said to truly age. It may even be said, in view of the role
played by lysosomes in the turnover process, that the aging
of lysosomes is the price cells have to pay for rejuvenating
their other constituents.

How big is the price? In other words, is this progressive
overloading of the lysosomes harmful to the cells? Does it
play a significant role in cellular senescence? The genetic
storage diseases provide us with an interesting and il-
luminating answer to the first question. In many of these
diseases, the same basic pathogenic mechanism is opera-
tive: directly attributable to the genetic anomaly, there is a
severe deficiency of one of the lysosomal enzymes. Con-
sequently, all the substances that require this enzyme at
some step of their digestion in the lysosomes find themselves arrested at the degradative stage where intervention by the missing enzyme becomes necessary for digestion to continue. These undigestible materials pile up in

the lysosomes, which swell to enormous proportions. To date, this kind of pathogenic mechanism has been recognized, and the underlying biochemical defect identified in a number of different congenital storage diseases including Tay–Sachs, Niemann-Pick, Hurler, Hunter, Fabry, Gaucher, and Pompe diseases and a dozen lesser known similar conditions. Predictably the nature of the stored materials depends on that of the deficient enzyme; the clinical manifestations and evolution of the disease on the nature of the most afflicted cells and on the rapidity with which the stored materials accumulate. But common to all lysosomal storage diseases, are a progressive deterioration of cell structure and function associated with the lysosomal swelling and a fatal outcome generally within the first few years of life.

It seems reasonably sure from these experiments of nature, fortunately of rare occurrence, that overloading of the lysosomes is sufficient in itself to bring about severe cellular damage, to the point of causing lethal impairments of function. This is particularly true in neurons, where lack of expansion space causes any increase in lysosome volume necessarily to take place at the expense of other cell constituents.

To evaluate fully the relevance of these observations to the aging problem, we need to know the quantitative relationship that exists between the proportion of total cytoplasmic volume occupied by the lysosomes and the severity of the resulting cellular deficiencies. The relationship could be one of fairly simple proportionality, in which case lysosome overloading could indeed play a significant role in cellular senescence. On the other hand, we could be dealing with some sort of threshold form of relationship, according to which cellular deficiencies start manifesting themselves only when the lysosomal volume exceeds a certain fraction of the cytoplasmic volume. This threshold may never be reached under normal conditions, in which case lysosome overloading must be considered simply a concomitant of aging, without any causal involvement in the process of senescence.

The question thus remains open. For the present, there is enough circumstantial evidence to make a possible participation of lysosomes in aging worth keeping in mind. Particularly intriguing is the possibility that lysosome overloading may in some way be responsible for the impairment in the autophagic clearance of defective molecules, evoked above as a possible cause of the accumulation of such molecules. There are, of course, many other ways in which swollen lysosomes could contribute to cell and tissue damage. They can be more liable than normal lysosomes to spill out their enzymes intracellularly or extracellularly. They can fail to perform adequately some of the manifold functions they subserve in addition to autophagy. Finally, there is the simple fact that when lysosomes grow bigger in cells that occupy an unexpandable space, other important organelles necessarily become reduced in a similar proportion.

References

Gershon, H. and Gershon, D. Inactive enzyme molecules in aging mice: liver aldolase. *Proceedings National Academy of Science*, 1973, *70*, 909–913.

Holliday, R. and Tarrant, G. M. Altered enzymes in aging human fibroblasts. *Nature*, 1972, *238*, 26–30.

Orgel, L. E. The maintenance of the accuracy of protein synthesis and its relevance to aging. *Proceedings National Academy of Science*, 1963, *49*, 517–521.

Beyond the bright searchlights of science,
Out of sight of the windows of sense,
Old riddles still bid us defiance,
Old questions of Why and of Whence.

William Cecil Dempier Whetham
The Recent Development of Physical Science 1904, p 10

3

THE "METABOLIC CODE"—
A Key To
Prolonging Life?

GORDON M. TOMKINS*

This discussion explores the possible dynamics by which primitive cells evolved biological regulatory mechanisms, and how such mechanisms could have laid the foundation for the meaningful communication between cells, at least at the molecular level. These considerations lead to speculation about the origin of the nervous system and may, therefore, include significance for aspects of communication between organisms as well as cells.

First, I assume that life began as macromolecular assemblies exhibiting simple cyclical chemical activities, forerunners of modern cellular metabolism. Such systems probably arose and decomposed until evolutionary

*This chapter is published posthumously, based on the original manuscript and a subsequent publication in Science (1976), editorial changes having been kept to a minimum. Dr. Keith Yamamoto's assistance in providing manuscripts and reading the chapter is gratefully acknowledged.

changes assured their self-replication. An energy crisis was one of the serious problems to which such an assembly would have made an adaptation. Similar to contemporary society, a primitive metabolic assembly could have survived only as long as the metabolic substrates required for energy and macromolecular synthesis were available. For instance, in the absence of glucose, these assemblies could not generate energetic intermediates like ATP (adenosine triphosphate), and in the absence of such energy they would disintegrate.

As is still the case in modern times, an essential element required for the survival of primitive cells would seem to be the development of "early warning systems" which would signal the potential exhaustion of a required nutrient. Since different nutrients play their individual roles in modern metabolism, it is likely that the same situation obtained in primitive times. Therefore, an essential feature of such a warning system would have been a specific signal generated in response to each type of nutritional deficiency. Although the details of the generation of such signals can never be known, plausible molecular models based on contemporary biochemistry can be constructed. B. N. Ames of the University of California, Berkeley, designated such signals as *alarmones*.

Two examples of substances of this type are currently under intensive study in many molecular biology laboratories. One is the omnipresent cyclic nucleotide, cyclic AMP, a symbol for carbon-source starvation, the concentration of which increases when bacterial cells are starved of glucose. A second such compound is a guanosine tetraphosphate, ppGpp, sometimes referred to as Magic Spot 1. This substance is formed when bacterial cells are starved of an amino acid normally required for growth. Thus, each compound symbolizes a specific nutritional lack. Using this information, a "metabolic code" can be envisaged in which a particular nutritional or metabolic crisis, such as glucose or amino acid starvation, is represented by an appropriate, more or less specific, intracellular molecular symbol.

The actions of cyclic AMP and ppGpp as metabolic symbols are instructive examples of how intracellular regulatory programs are organized. Both of the compounds interact, directly or indirectly, with a large number of specific cellular components, producing a coordinated metabolic response appropriate to the specific nutritional lack they symbolize.

While ppGpp interacts both with genetic and other cellular components, the chemical interactions of cyclic AMP are all at the genetic level—in bacteria. In either case, each symbol "calls" a complex program whose elements consist of changes in various cellular functions designed by evolutionary selection to facilitate metabolic adaptation to the specific deficiency state.

A later state in evolution probably involved communication of a deficiency state from one cell to another. This interaction might well have begun by transmission of the symbol itself into the surrounding medium as the result of a chance event, e.g., failure of a "producer cell" variant to respond to one of its own internal symbols because of accidental mutational events. It is relatively easy to generate such mutant cells in the laboratory today.

Thus, it is hypothesized that if such an extracellular regulatory molecule encountered another cell capable of responding to it, then it might, in turn, liberate substances which would relieve the deficiency in the sender cell. If then, by chance, the responder cell had been unable to generate the symbol, an obligatory two-element communication network would have been established. The maintenance of such a network would have survival value for both elements. Encounters of this type may have been important for the evolution of multi-cellular organisms.

There is for example, the cellular slime mold, in which individual cells, when starved, generate cyclic AMP and then discharge it into the medium, where it affects the behavior of surrounding cells. Since the response to an intracellular symbol may be quite complex, the response to a transmitted symbol may likewise be an entire set of coordinated adaptive reactions. In the slime mold, these responses lead to cellular differentiation, triggered by cyclic AMP.

It seems most likely that hormones, which mediate intercellular transactions in modern organisms, arose as second-order symbols representing the original intracellular signals. Such a development might have been favored because of the inherent instability of the intracellular mediators, an instability which may be important for their normal biological function.

In present day organisms, cyclic AMP is generated by many cells as a result of the interaction of specific hormones with their membranes. Metabolic coding may, therefore, involve not only the primary association between nutritional deprivation and a particular symbol, but also secondary coupling in which the primary symbol becomes associated with a secondary one, presumably better adapted for intercellular transmission.

These views suggest rather simple generalizations about the complexities of intercellular communication. Ordinarily, particular cell types respond in a characteristic way and only to specific, externally applied chemical stimuli such as hormones, drugs, antigens and embryonic "inducers." It is not understood, in detail, how a number of hormones of diverse chemical structure interact with their "target cells" to generate cell-specific and hormone-specific responses. For example, adrenocorticotropic hormone (ACTH) stimulates adrenal cells to produce their characteristic steroids. Thyroid-stimulating hormone (TSH) likewise specifically activates thyroid cells to produce thyroxin. Neither of the stimulatory hormones affects the target cells of the other. Therefore, these two transactions appear to be totally unrelated. At the molecular level, however, both adrenocorticotropic and thyroid-stimulating hormones have identical actions. Both promote the synthesis of a common intracellular symbol, cyclic AMP, often called a "second messenger" in this context. Cyclic AMP, within the target cells, by interaction with cell-specific components produces a characteristic response and it seems very likely that similar, or closely related, mechanisms apply to other cell-effector reactions as well. These considerations suggest that the metabolic code, like the genetic code, has an aspect of universality.

The assumption is that each cell "knows" what to do with a particular symbol to bring about the appropriate cellular event, and, indeed, different cells are programmed to respond differently to the same internal symbol. This programming is carried out by the chromosomes, which allow only certain types of protein molecules to be present in particular cells, the constellation of intracellular proteins determining not only the form and function of each cell, but also its response to a particular symbolic molecule, such as cyclic AMP.

This formulation has implications for developmental biology as well as for the field of intracellular communication. Generally speaking, there are two broad theories of development. The first implies that primitive cells are undifferentiated and develop into specific cell types in response to external factors. In this view, the external influences must carry information on how the cell is to develop. The second theory states that there are no "undifferentiated" cells, but that each cell has a characteristic state of differentiation, determined by its array of protein components. In this view, external effectors direct development by eliciting the production of one or more of the "universal metabolic symbols"; the cell, by virtue of its state of differentiation, responds appropriately. Thus, for example, cyclic AMP generated intracellularly could induce an intestinal cell to develop into a pancreatic cell, as well as stimulating adrenal cells to produce steroids.

Speculations of this kind suggest hypotheses about the origin of the nervous system. I assume that specific metabolic symbols arose in response to particular nutritional stresses. Furthermore, the transmission of these symbols or their secondary manifestations, the hormones, developed to communicate metabolic information from one cell to another to facilitate adaptation to metabolic stress. Neural transmitters are, of course, interneural hormones and it seems likely that they enhanced metabolic adaptation by adding to the repertoire of chemical responses, changes in electrical conductance and, therefore, the possibility of responses based on more rapid transmission.

This presentation has been an attempt to formulate a model for the origin and function of chemical communication between cells. It supposes that an initial evolutionary event was the establishment of a more or less universal "metabolic code" in which specific intracellular symbols came to represent particular nutritional deficiency states. Hormones are postulated to have arisen as second-order "coding" events, allowing molecules more stable than the original intracellular symbols to be transmitted from cell to cell. These ideas suggest that many cellular changes (development, antibody production, etc.) are due to intracellular modulations of relatively few symbolic molecules. Furthermore, it is suggested that the nervous system arose as an extension of metabolic adaptation. The neural transmitters themselves might represent metabolic states and individual pathways could have arisen as independent adaptations to particular deficiencies.

The development of the nervous system and metabolic adaptation also suggest a relationship to aging. To date, there is one interesting hypothesis to account for aging at the cellular level: the error catastrophe theory of Orgel. Recent experiments, however, suggest that aging may not result from an accumulation of incorrectly assembled macro-molecules as Orgel's theory suggests. Instead, aging may represent a condition of abnormal responsiveness to metabolic symbols. A great deal of contemporary cell biology is devoted to studies showing that overall cell functions can be controlled by symbolic substances such as those discussed above. It is likely, therefore, that such interactions will presently be much better understood. If that be the case, it seems, for better or worse, life can be prolonged. Let us hope that the state of the world does not make a mockery of such optimism.

References

Many of the ideas on the role of these indicator molecules in bacterial cells originated from discussions with B. N. Ames. He calls these molecules "alarmones" (Stephens, J. C., Artz, S. W., and Ames, B. N.: N. Proc. Natl. Acad. Sci. U.S.A., in press) and considers them in detail in Ames, B. N. and Artz, S. W., in preparation. (Comment of Gordon Tomkins.)

Barkley, D. S. Adenosine 3', 5'-phosphate: identification as acrosin in a specie of cellular slime mold. *Science*, 1969, *165*, 1133.

Cashel, M. J. The control of ribonucleic acid synthesis in *escherichia coli* IV Reliance of unusual phosphorylated compounds from amino-acid starved strains. *Journal of Biological Chemistry*, 1969, *244*, 3133.

Cashel, M. J., & Gallant, T. J. Two compounds implicated in the function of the RC gene of *escherichia coli*. *Nature*, 1969, *221*, 838.

Cashel, M. J., & Kalbacher, B. The control of ribonucleic acid synthesis in *escherichia coli*, characterization of a nucleotide associated with a stringent response. *Journal of Biological Chemistry*, 1970, *245*, 2309.

Emmer, M., Crombrugge, B., Pastan, I., & Perlman, R. *Proceedings of the National Academy of Science*, United States, 1970, *66*, 480.

Fleischer, N., Donald, R. A., & Butcher, R. W. Involvement of adenosine 3', 5'-monophosphate in release of ACTH. *American Journal of Physiology*, 1969, *217*, 1287.

Konijn, T. M. Effect of Bacteria on Chemotaxis in the Cellular Slime Molds. *Journal of Bacteriology*, 1969, *99*, 503.

Waddington, C. H. *Organizers and Genes*, London: Cambridge University Press, 1940.

Wilber, J. F., Peake, G. T., & Utiger, R. D. Thyrotropin release in vitro: stimulation by cyclic 3', 5'-adenosine monophosphate. *Endocrinology*, 1969, *84*, 758.

Woese, C. R. *The Genetic Code*. New York: Harper & Row, 1967.

Zubay, G., Schwartz, D., & Beckwith, J. Mechanism of activation of catabolite-sensitive genes: A positive control system. *Proceedings of the National Academy of Science*, United States, 1970, *66*, 480.

4

A BIOLOGIST LAMENTS AND EXHORTS

ALEXANDER COMFORT

The most immediate gerontological problem facing the developed countries is not that of physical aging, but of "sociogenic" age imposed upon healthy, intelligent, sexual, and employable persons by a combination of folklore about the effects of physical aging and the imposition of arbitrary roles, or rather rolelessness, upon seniors. "The old" in America resemble blacks and women upon whom social prejudice has imposed arbitrary and unjust limitations and who have come at times to believe in the inherency of the barriers erected against them by vulgar ignorance. Wholly baseless notions of decline in work capacity and intelligence, as well as in sexual capacity, have patterned the expectations of older people. Belied in two world wars by a return of "the old" to active employment, these prejudices returned with peace while barriers against women and Blacks were pushed back, because, unlike stable groups in the community, "the old" turn over, and the newly old have to refight the same battles against prejudice and their own expectations. A greater social awareness and better information of the more numerous "old," who have enforced leisure and are registered voters, is bound to lead to increasingly vociferous protest against ejection from life and relegation to a play-space. Retirement will be increasingly seen as what it is—compulsory unemployment. This will be the first battleground of future gerontological policy since it is the most easily altered.

In this chapter I will confine myself to the control of real, not socially imaginary age changes—those which impair physical health and can be attacked only by physical means. In forming a new society these are the less immediate changes we may expect, but they are fundamental to science policy. Science may affect human longevity favorably in two ways—by suppressing causes of premature death, or by postponing the aging process which causes our liability to disease and death to increase logarithmically with the passage of time. The first of these two influences has already meant that in privileged countries more and more people reach the so-called "specific age," 75 to 80 years, without altering that age range appreciably. The second, which is now in the stage of active research, aims at postponement or slowing of the aging process itself.

It is highly important to recognize the difference between this approach, based on the search for a systems breakthrough, and the sum of all the other sociomedical advances. The large changes in the survival curve of Man over the last century represent, quite simply, the removal of causes of premature death; but the age at which a person becomes old, judged by the criteria of growing infirmity and growing liability to die, is exactly what it was in Biblical times. Aging itself, in the sense employed by gerontologists, is a process which results in an increasing instability with time. This "loss of information" is multiform, but its rate, measured by the force of mortality, is highly stable and the increase is roughly logarithmic. This stability is the basis of the well-justified assurance of actuaries that, premature causes of death apart, an annuitant will die between the ages of 70 and 100 years, regardless of any advance in the cure or prevention of specific diseases. There is, in fact, a biological limit on human longevity which cannot be much transcended by conventional improvements in medicine or living conditions.

Biological interference with the actual rate of aging, however, will be ready for trial in Man as soon as "aging rates" can be made measurable in the individual and in the short term, thereby avoiding impracticable experiments lasting 70 to 80 years. It is virtually certain that such experiments will be begun within the next decade.

The effect of success in transferring existing rodent techniques to Man would be that a treated subject of about 80 would have, for a ten-year gain, the same health and the same disabilities he or she would have had at age 70. The likely prediction, based on rodent work and on radiation life-shortening, is that by affecting the rate of aging most of the changes in a given individual could be postponed roughly "across the board," i.e., both tumors and pedestrian accidents would occur at later ages. Resistant processes such as glaucoma, caused by continued growth of the eye lens, may have to picked off singly. The period of senility would not be prolonged and, ideally, preadolescent development would not be lengthened.

In the broader medico-social view, the argument for seeking a systems breakthrough depends on these facts: (1) Longer vigorous adult life cannot be achieved in any other way in view of the multiple nature of the expressions of aging in Man; removal of single causes of death will only expose others already present. (2) On present evidence the project appears to be feasible. (3) It is easier to affect a rate than to rewrite a biological program; accordingly, it will probably be much easier to postpone cancer, or atheroma for example, than to prevent or reverse them. (4) Other specific medical research directed to single diseases, while extremely necessary, will find many of its tasks subsumed in any general understanding of aging. (5) It is extremely likely that an empirical means of slowing human aging will appear before any complete readback of the exact processes involved.

Forecasting is accordingly possible. Direct experiment on the delaying of age changes in Man is virtually certain to be in hand within the next decade, probably at more than one center. If the techniques used in rodents prove directly applicable, or if we are lucky, some agent demonstrably reducing the rate of mature human aging is likely to be known within 15 years. The likely amount of such an increase, on the rodent analogy, could well be 10% to 20%. The limit of possible increase is not predictable at present, bearing in mind that each increase gives additional time for research to bear fruit. This represents the lower limit of speed in development, given the present small investment, about $7,500,000 in the United States (Prehoda, 1968). If rodent-type procedures fail to affect human aging when started in adult life, or if the postponement of age changes is partial, unequal, or accompanied by unforeseen effects the rate of future progress will depend increasingly on the amount of research investment. However, once the machinery and experience for direct human experiment has been created, rapid application of new knowledge directly to Man can be envisaged. The creation of this machinery for use with basically harmless procedures is the next priority in research planning.

The technical approaches to age control now foreseen are various and depend on a number of hypotheses on the nature of aging, so far unconfirmed, which have been described in other papers (Comfort, 1968, in press). Earlier predictions emphasized the use of techniques based upon calorie restriction, molecular protection by antioxidants, and other empirical approaches, on the assumption that given an observed change in the rate of rodent or human aging, we are more likely to discover the causes of aging processes by seeing what alters them than by the inductive reverse. More recent work, however, suggests that this may not be the case. The nonspecific or cellular theories of aging are apparently being replaced, or at least supplemented, by a conception of accessible lifespan programming located in the hypothalamus, upon which caloric restriction and other known antisenile agents most probably act. The earlier probability, that human age would prove to be timed by molecular biology, is replaced, in the light of recent work (Finch, 1976), by a model directed first to the search for a hypothalamic "clock," presumably driven by changes in neuroendocrines, accessible to the action of dietary factors (especially tryptophan levels) of monoamines such as L-DOPA and monoamine oxidase

inhibitors, and to interference on the output side by identification of its actions on releaser oligopeptides. There are
clearly many possible routes of access to such a mechanism
if it exists; it may even be possible to influence its performance by purely psychoneurological methods, such as
biofeedback. Such an aging "clock" mechanism almost certainly times the end of human reproductive life and the
observed age changes in hormone turnover. Since its function would be to integrate lifespan, it must accordingly be
capable of overriding or timing cellular and other local
aging processes, although these in the free-running state
are likely to have their own preferred rate and to be expressed eventually as causes of dyshomeostasis if the overriding clock is much slowed. There is, accordingly, a
strong probability that the aging which we should observe,
with maximal interference directed to such a clock, may be
quite different from its present pattern and be expressed,
for example, in exhaustion of cell division. Resetting the
clock, if there is one, would alter only the scale of the
present life cycle. Anything further is science fiction. Both
the limits of clock resetting and the kind of aging we would
then observe are quite unpredictable.

Research, however, is likely to continue into methods
of controlling cellular and local age mechanisms, bearing
in mind that the neuroendocrine shift which appears to
time the clock may itself be of this kind. Here the method
of interference selected, such as dietary restriction,
neurohormone administration, immunotherapy, administration of drugs, molecular protectants, metabolic regu-
lators, biofeedback manipulations, or hormones, will be
theoretically determined; utility will not necessarily depend on the correctness of the hypothesis. The Wasser-

mann reaction for syphilis, which is a keystone of preventive medicine, was developed on a wholly erroneous assumption, and its exact mode of action is still not fully know.

All in all, the following assumptions seem justified: (1) that by the year 2000 we shall know of a testable way of slowing aging; (2) that the agents involved will be simple and cheap and will not depend, for example, on elaborate intensive-care units, large physical apparatus, or transplants of major organs; (3) that the direct application of the research will be possible at about the same rate as the application of worldwide antibiotics; and (4) that all existing medical services and governments will elect to apply them or at least be unable to prevent their application. Accordingly, we had better get used to the idea. The main reservation on likely application is where longevity depends on prolonged and tiresome dietary restriction. The model of cigarette-induced life shortening and coronary diseases suggests that public concern for longevity does not extend to making oneself uncomfortable. However, in this event, research on agents inhibiting calorie absorption or further breakdown of the nature of the diet effect, which almost certainly operates via a neuroendocrine mechanism, would probably soon render the method acceptable.

Implications of Success

Our discussion of the implications of success in modifying the rate of aging should preferably be based on this realistic model, rather than on wild estimates of 200- to

300-year survival in the remote future. Considerations in altering the aging rate are demographic, economic, political, psychological, and philosophical, with substantial overlap. Our assessment of them depends, moreover, on some examination of current attitudes to aging, lifespan, and the elderly in American culture—the society at present most likely to achieve the required systems breakthrough. Once achieved in the United States or in Europe, in Russia or in Japan, the option of application would immediately become worldwide.

We can probably make the following assumptions: (1) Postponement of aging is unlikely to include the abolition of eventual "old age," which will simply happen later. The Aldous Huxley model of 70 years of apparent youth followed by sudden death is biologically unlikely. (2) Any technique of longevity production involving diapause, gross prolongation of childhood, or eventual prolongation of senility is unlikely to be generally adopted. (3) Once one major systems breakthrough is achieved, there is a fair chance of feedback, wider understanding of process, and further bonuses. (4) From the moment that systems breakthrough is achieved, past actuarial experience is no longer predictively serviceable.

Demographically, longer life will involve an increase in population. Assuming that increased years do not lead to increased family size and that there is only one such increment, this increase will be temporary, though the "bulge" will appear at the time when world population problems are likely to be maximal. The increase in total world population by the year 2020 from gerontological manipulations is unlikely, in a reasonable scenario, to exceed 7% (Prehoda, 1970). On the other hand, the gain envisaged is wholly in the productive, nondependent years. At present, in any occupation, preproductive life occupies plus or minus 20 years and postproductive life plus or minus 15 to 20 years. Moreover, education is becoming longer and, in privileged countries, retirement begins earlier. A gain of 20% in the total lifespan, of the kind envisaged here, would represent a 40% gain in the total nondependent or employed lifespan. How important this would be to subsistence economies is not clear. Its utility for cultures which compulsorily retire workers at their age of maximum experience and efficiency will depend on a willingness to undergo a major change of attitude. This, however, is already overdue without any further scientific advance.

The number of Americans aged 65 years or older is now over 20 million. By 2000 this number will increase to approximately 30 million (United States Bureau of the Census, 1973, 1976; cf. McFarland, this volume). The number of dependent children and students is also likely to increase. In the 21st century, the proportion of the lifespan over which each citizen remains a potential contributor to the economy will depend very largely upon education and retirement policy and upon the results of gerontological research.

The financial results of a possible systems breakthrough seem to have been insufficiently realized: It would remove the present "floor" under actuarial calculations. Whether the gain on insurance from non-decease of life policy holders will offset the losses from increased survival of annuitants, only the life insurance offices can calculate. Existing pensions schemes are already outrunning the calculations on which they were based. Although it is no part of the biologist's duty to determine premiums on insurance, I know of only one British life insurance office which incorporates into its pension proposal form a waiver of rate in the event of a major change in the expectation of life. So far, more anxiety has been shown by American offices over the use of such shenanigans as "cryonic suspension" and possibly vexatious litigation than over the real biological possibilities which I have outlined.

The psychological, political, and philosophical implications of a gain in longevity are less easy to assess. It is evident that longer life involves a slower turnover both of persons in office and of generations. Oriental courtiers were traditionally able to say "O King, live forever!" in the knowledge that every personal tyranny has its term. More significant than the longer potential duration of that term is the fact that, with a slower turnover and a maintained rate of technological change, the discrepancy between learned attitudes and actuality, now reflected both in politics and in the "generation gap," will be increased. It is not clear how far adaptability is an inherent and therefore biologically modifiable characteristic or how much it depends upon social roles. A tenure of office for administrators, executives, or professors increased by 40% cannot be viewed with total complacency. The risks have been brilliantly assessed by Harvey Wheeler (1970). It is also probable that the present "generation gap," which goes considerably beyond the normally mutual incomprehension of parents and children, is a product of the fact that the rate of total change in lifestyle, caused by technology is now of the order of one (unmodified) generation, our own being probably the first generation where this has been so. Aggravation of this gap, of the discrepancy between modern conditions and the training of 20 or 30 years ago, and of that between modern needs and political positions adopted 20 or 30 years ago, will, like the problems of promotion-structure with longer life, be temporary in the long term as the "tail" catches up. However, the initial adjustment to an increased and potentially open-ended lifespan will require efforts in social adaptability of which at present we show little sign.

The psychological implications of a demonstrable breach in the age-barrier are even less calculable. We do not know what proportion of human unconscious attitudes are determined by the awareness, not only of eventual death—which is postponed into fantasy—but of the certainty of eventual death at a fixed time, i.e., the knowledge that there is a year in which it is reasonably certain that we shall not be alive. The relation of this time scale to life style, to affect (capacity to experience hope for the future and experience depression or regression as this hope becomes limited), and to the "shape" of unconscious development has been somewhat neglected by psychoanalysts. The fact of a breakthrough may, in this context, be more significant than its size; if decline can be postponed once, the fantasy that it may be postponed indefinitely acquires a new permission. The importance of the awareness of eventual death, recognized by writers such as Unamuno more fully perhaps than by psychiatrists, has almost certainly been underrated, and any change in this pattern might produce profound emotional effects. These are likely to be more fundamental than the present changes induced by higher survival to old age, which include the appearance of a second, adolescence-type identity crisis around the age of 45.

I do not want to enlarge on this highly speculative consideration, except insofar as it has a direct bearing on research priorities. Scientific research in modern societies, so far from being rationally directed, has taken on some of the functions performed in primitive societies by shamanic magic; and much of it appears to the anthropological observer to be fueled by unconscious fantasies. Travel to the moon is one such shamanic fantasy made literal at huge expense. Indefinite prolongation of life is another. Though feasible prolongation is unlikely to be indefinite in this sense, the whole subject closely approaches an archetypal fantasy which our society may be about to enact. This would be of theoretical interest only if the allocation of research funds did not depend substantially upon considerations of this kind.

The philosophical implications of increased longevity are outside my field, but there are certain points about the philosophy of aging research which are of direct practical relevance to medicine. It would represent the first major instance of which I am aware in which science can be said to produce an artificial betterment of biological function, as against the best observed natural performance. More important, perhaps, is the possibility of anguished and unproductive argument between a naturalist view (that turnover is a good in itself which should not be resisted by the individual out of a selfish desire to survive), and the general humanist position that the quintessence of respect for people is to preserve them as individuals as long as possible. This argument has been obscured in the past by the imperfect character of the attainable preservation.

Fortunately for the humanist view, which I, for unconscious as well as conscious reasons, hold to be the right one, the Rubicon of an initial systems breakthrough is highly likely to be passed before the argument becomes general, so that, as in the case of birth control, Hudibrastic arguments will come too late and the public will vote with its feet. By far the most likely moral effect of greater longevity now with the prospect of further longevity later will be a large enhancement of respect for life, based on respect for our own skin. Concomitantly, there will be a comparably enhanced respect for death—our own and other people's—attributable to the decline in the conviction of spiritual immortality.

I mention these general considerations, not to resolve them, but because it would be culpable to devote oneself to gerontological research without bearing them in mind. They also influence the likelihood of research support, application of results, and society's choice of priorities. More important, perhaps, in all projections of the future and the use of such research is the present condition of the old in developed countries. This has unconscious origins in the attitudes I have defined and leads to the conclusion that for most consumers, abolition of "old age" as it is now seen, although biomedically far more remote, would be an even higher priority than vigorous longer life followed by a normally patterned old age.

Old Age in Developed Societies

To a humane person who has had the opportunity to observe it extensively rather than in selected vigorous individuals, and especially in our society, which notably mistreats the old, the existence fantasized as old age—the progressive extinction of strength, skills, well-being, and the sense of futurity—is not tolerable. The old in all cultures undergo some biological loss; but our own culture adds to them a self-fulfilling prophecy of decline, whereas many of the simpler societies provide compensations. These compensations of status, respect, authority, magical attributes, and guiltless dependence are wholly denied to the old in privileged cultures, of which Britain and the United States are models. To the biological losses are added, in our society, loss of role, activity, self-esteem, and social worth, quite unrelated to the limited physical decrements of normal, healthy aging. The dependence which, in age-reverencing cultures, is gladly accepted as a right, is a source of consuming guilt and fruitless effort as well as isolation among the technopolitan old. It is considered a violation of the independence value-system to live with children or grandchildren. The anthropology of this added group of deprivations has been set forth in a study by Kalish (1969). Virtually all modern Anglo-American values militate against any kind of social compensation for the biological deficits of being old. In this culture, accordingly, the old can rightly be regarded as a disadvantaged group. They are exposed to the attacks of natural senescence, the effects of inflation, and the pressures of socioanthropological attitudes to dependence, modernity, and achievement which, for us, is always prospective: past achievement does not score. There is, as well, a whole battery of unconscious fears among the non-old ranging from stereotype formation to active dislike by the physician who has come to depend upon activism as a defense mechanism against his early encounters with suffering. Such a man experiences the incurable and the old as threatening and castrating objects (Comfort, 1967). The pattern of attitude to the old—stereotype, covert prejudice, fear, economic disadvantage, role-played "oldness," dependence-thinking, attempts at segregation —has close analogies to the situation of the Black. This comparison, though close, is also remarkable. If there were as many rich, powerful and administratively decision-making Blacks as there are rich, powerful and decision-making old and aging men, Black Power would long ago have been a reality. One wonders why the old men in office do so little about using their power for the old. Moreover, people are born black or poor or immigrant and may transcend it, but we shall all become old. Possibly the answer lies in rejection of a cultural stereotype of old age by the influential old, a response which needs to become more general, and in removal of an emotional block in the young toward realistic considerations of their own future. The rejection of age by the prosperous old may be like the occasional rejection of blackness by the successful Black, or of immigrant origin by the successful foreign-born.

So long as this attitude persists in tandem with the real biological deficits of age, the equally real measures taken by health administrations to palliate the rejections of old people are inevitably tainted with pollyannaism and the kind of patronizing consideration we show to pets or the subnormal. Moreover, the cultural attitude, though it may be changed or may change of itself, has in a sense pushed our estimate of aging beyond a point of no return: expectation has changed. Restitution of the old-style social and religious compensations would not now do. Our model of "old age" has been seen to be intolerable; it is now obligatory for our culture to see if it is also preventable. This attitude, which has been brashly but forcibly stated by Harrington (1969), is likely to set the key for future societies even if we relearn how to treat the old in a civilized way.

Technological forecasters refer to the point at which a theoretically attainable goal is seen to be practically feasible as the Hahn–Strassmann point, from the analogy of the demonstration of nuclear fission. The curve of subsequent development from that point consists of a number of envelopes determined chiefly by the amount of financial investment in the subject (Prehoda, 1968); even at the lowest level of investment, however, the goal—in this case a 15% to 20% prolongation of the human presenile period—is likely to be attained eventually. Although gerontology is now a worldwide study, only the United States possesses the resources in volume and the quality of biological research to implement this possibility at the highest attainable rate, in combination with anthropological, unconscious, and attitudinal drives in its public and leaders which make such a maximal effort likely. It is, in other words, the country where dissatisfaction with the existing lifespan is combined with the pragmatism necessary to attack problems practically. Confidence in science remains the American resource in the face of overriding human desires of this kind. A growth in humane concern and a rejection of stereotypes is most likely to divert the direction of scientific effort into a realization of needs.

In the long term, a society based on increased lifespan and low turnover would be stable. Since reduction in reproductive rate is now a worldwide necessity, whether or not gerontology succeeds in prolonging adult vigor, this looks like the pattern of the future: Zero population growth demands long-term people. So far, the model has attracted little predictive attention. Contingency planning of this kind and action by scientists to prevent the abuse or distortion of the outcome by commercially or politically-motivated groups is already overdue. Such abuse could be paternalistic suppression, or denial of medical advances to unpopular or exploited sections of mankind, or the confinement of medical advances by power-holders, either deliberately or through the maintenance of a more general worldwide social injustice. If the potentiality of longer life exacerbates the demand for human equality, it will only add to an irresistible demand for an end of exploitation and the fair division of all resources.

The scenario used by Prehoda (1970) envisages two additive increments in vigorous longevity, each of 15%. One is cheap and simple, the other complex and costly. Taking the models of penicillin use and kidney grafting, and their application worldwide by developed and underdeveloped countries, it is possible to forecast a gerontology-dependent increase of 7% overall in world population by 2020. Other scenarios would yield other results. In most such forecasts, the concentration of extra longevity would be chiefly in privileged societies and is insignificant compared with the natural population increase expected from falling child mortality and the slow application of medical research and social justice in the developing countries. Accordingly, we need to look at the realities of future research beyond the immediate prospect: postponement of the senile decline. They appear to be these:

1. Postponement of the onset of present-type old age by 10% to 20% will not reduce the duration of oldness or, probably, its pattern of disability. It will, however, almost certainly throw enough light on the aging process to make future extrapolation possible for subsequent pattern-modifying activities.

2. Large postponement of 50% to 100% might reduce the sense of urgency in this field by cutting the size of the cohort at risk, the postponees relying on "something turning up" during their enhanced lifespan in the general course of research.

3. Palliative geriatrics, which offer a high but insufficient measure of relief to those now old, must not be squeezed out by any large investment in longevity research. On the other hand, the old will eventually benefit from any available research information.

4. The reversibility of existing age changes is difficult to forecast and likely to be less wholesale than postponement, since, for example, lost cells may be irreplaceable by conventional methods. If the information loss with aging is molecular and affects the primary copies, e.g., in DNA, the likelihood of simple reversal is small. If, however, it occurs later in the chain, at the synthetase level as proposed by Orgel (1965), then in theory, at least, recourse to the intact primary copies might reverse some or all established age changes. It should be clear within 10 years or sooner whether this theoretical possibility exists.

5. It is impossible to forecast either the length or the completeness of the postponement I have described. The

time and pattern of its running out will determine the efficacy of special measures such as organ grafts, cultured prostheses, etc., which may then be available. These will, in any event, be expensive and elaborate techniques which would raise intensely embarrassing issues of priorities, privilege, and human aims in general—the issues I have outlined as not yet urgent in connection with postponement technology. Indefinite postponement is conceivable but unlikely to be total; i.e., some deteriorative changes are almost bound to resist it and require it to be dealt with separately. Truly indefinite postponement, enthusiastically but rashly forecast by some futurologists, would involve having a population in which only stochastic or deliberate deaths occurred, with demographic consequences quite different from those of a general, limited longevity increase and with severe problems over reproductivity and replacement. This is not yet an issue, although having achieved one postponement we would have absolutely no means of predicting its possible further extension save by trial. We may do well, therefore, to give these issues some preliminary thought, since the likelihood is that our cultural sense of the intolerability of aging, which is a branch of our sense of the intolerability of death, has probably come to stay.

References

Comfort, A. On gerontophobia. *Medical Opinion Review*, 1967, *3*, 30–37.

Comfort, A. Feasibility in age research. *Nature*, 1968, *217*, 320–322.

Comfort, A. *Aging, the Biology of Senescence*, 3rd edition. Amsterdam: Elsevier, in press.

The dependencies of old people. R. A. Kalish (Ed.), *Occasional Papers on Gerontology*, 1969, University of Michigan Institute of Gerontology, Wayne State University, Michigan.

Finch, C. E. The regulation of physiological changes during mammalian aging. *Quarterly Review of Biology*, 1976, *51*, 49–83.

Harrington, A. The *Immortalists*. New York: Random House, 1969.

Kohn, R. Human aging and disease. *Journal of Chronic Diseases*, 1963, *16*, 5–21.

Logan, R. F. L., and Agate, J. N. *Medicine in Old Age*. London: Pitman, 1965.

Mikat, B. Anstieg der Lebenserwartung der über-65-Jahrigen im internationalen Vergleich. *Gerontologia (Zurich)*, 1969, *2*, 201–203.

Orgel, L. E. The maintenance of the accuracy of protein synthesis and its relevance to aging. *Proceedings of the National Academy of Science*, 1965, *49*, 517–521.

Prehoda, R. W. *Designing the Future—the Role of Technological Forecasting*. Philadelphia: Chilton, 1967.

Prehoda, R. W. Proceedings of a conference on the social implications of the life-span change. Center for the Study of Democratic Institutions, Santa Barbara, California, 1970.

Wheeler, H. The rise of the elders. Saturday Evening Post, May 5, 1970, pp. 14–15, 42–43.

5

NUTRITION AND AGING:
Are We What We've Eaten?

ROSLYN B. ALFIN-SLATER and RUTH FRIEDMAN

It has often been said that people are reflections of what they eat. No doubt elderly persons with long-standing, well-established nutritional patterns are composites of many things which have occurred in their past—of diets which may or may not have been entirely nutritionally satisfactory, of eating habits which may or may not have provoked minor or major deficiencies, of past diseases which may or may not have affected their nutritional requirements. Also the nutritional status of the fetus *in utero* as well as the postnatal nutrition of the infant are parts of the total nutritional history which affect the health of the elderly.

In addition, of course, many nonnutritional factors affect the nutritional wellbeing of the aging population. These include cultural aspects of food selection, physical infirmities leading to decreased mobility which, in turn,

61

may interfere with the purchasing of food, and inadequate incomes with which to purchase sufficient quantities of good-quality foods. Some of these factors can be remedied by education and more attention to the problems of aging. Other problems will require governmental regulations and involve sociological and behavioral inputs as well.

The process of aging is poorly understood. It is known that aging is a complex biological process in which there is a reduced capacity for self-maintenance, i.e., a reduced ability to repair body cells. More cells are destroyed than are produced. In some tissues, e.g., in the brain, cells are simply destroyed without the formation of new ones. It is not known why these events occur with different speeds and different magnitudes, not only in different species of animals but also in different people. Why the turtle lives longer than the dog, the cat, the rat, or even the human is still in the realm of speculation. Furthermore, it is not understood why some people age prematurely, as in progeria, a form of pathological, premature senility in young children who show all the signs of extreme old age and die before they reach their tenth birthday. Also, we do not know why certain individuals appear to age more slowly and with fewer ill effects than others.

Nutritional Aspects of Longevity

Is there a nutritional component to longevity? Experiments with rats and certain protozoa have shown that aging can be delayed in these species by lowering the caloric intake as well as by lowering the temperature at appropriate times (Ross, 1964). Caloric restriction in young rats has prolonged their lifetime by as much as 50% (McCay et al., 1935, 1939). Longevity of chickens has been increased by keeping them immature as a result of omission of particular amino acids which were added later in the life cycle (Singsen et al., 1965; Couch & Tramwell, 1970).

Investigations have also looked at the diets of several reputed long-lived populations—the Hunzakuts of northern Pakistan, the Vilcabambians of Ecuador, and the Georgians in the Caucasus. Attempts to find a common denominator in their diets have not been successful. The Hunzakuts eat a low-calorie, low-animal-fat, vegetarian-type diet with dried apricots as a dietary staple, and practically no meat or dairy products. On the other hand, the Georgians eat a varied diet including meat, dairy products, sweets, and an abundance of vegetables. They also consume alcohol and tobacco. The Vilcabambians, like the Hunzakuts, subsist on a low-calorie, low-fat, vegetarian diet. However, they smoke and use alcohol and sugar liberally, as do the Georgians. Obviously these studies do not give us any information about a common nutritional deterrent to old age. What these populations do share, however, is a life of constant, vigorous activity.

Theories of Aging

According to one theory, aging is the result of increased oxidative reactions in the body and the accumulation of free radicals. (Free radicals are highly reactive molecules liberated during the lipid peroxidation of polyunsaturated fatty acids when these are unprotected by an antioxidant.) Because vitamin E at the cellular level has been shown to be an antioxidant as well as a free radical "scavenger," it is possible that vitamin E is indeed involved in some way in the aging process. Further support comes from experiments in which the addition of antioxidants, not necessarily vitamin E, to the diets of experimental animals has increased the mean lifespan (Harman, 1968; Tappel, 1968).

Other explanations for these observations include the fact that many antioxidants are also powerful hepatic enzyme inducers which may cause marked liver enlargement. A correlation between elevated hepatic enzyme concentrations and increased life expectancy has been observed. More research is needed on the possible relationship between antioxidants and life span.

Several other theories of aging describe cell death caused by the deterioration of deoxyribonucleic acid (Wulff et al., 1962), an impairment in protein synthesis caused by alterations in the synthetase enzyme (Medvedev, 1962), and the progressive breakdown of the immunological processes of body and intermolecular cross-linking of proteins or nucleic acids to produce large abnormal proteins (Ram, 1967). All of these theories require additional investigation, and all of them are consistent with nutritional influences on aging.

Present Problems of Nutrition in the Elderly

A thorough investigation needs to be made as to whether the majority of the elderly suffer from malnutrition. Indications of inadequate nutrition are slowly becoming available. A recent nutrition survey in this country (Ten State Survey, 1968, 1970) revealed that most older people, although not all, were indeed receiving sufficient protein. Problems did exist, however, with other nutrients: vitamin C, calcium, iron, folic acid, and, in some cases, other B vitamins, such as thiamine and vitamin B^{12}. Low-vitamin-C diets were found particularly in older males.

Most elderly people eat foods low in iron, a probable reflection of their high-carbohydrate diets, which are less expensive, require little or no preparation, and are easy to chew, even with dentures. Many older people also develop lactase deficiency, which prevents the digestion and absorption of the milk sugar, lactose, and since bloating and discomfort follow the ingestion of milk and dairy products, they learn to avoid these foods. However, milk and dairy products are excellent sources of calcium and the elimination of such foods may lead to calcium deficiency and its consequences. Low-lactase milk and other modified dairy products are now appearing on the market.

Nutrient insufficiencies, resulting from poor diets, from faulty absorption of nutrients, or both, are reflected in the ailments which presently plague our elderly population. For example, the low-calcium intake probably either causes or enhances osteoporosis. In this disease, which is more common in older women (especially in those women who have had children), painful fractures and even collapse of the decalcified bones of the back may occur. This seems primarily to be caused by lack of calcium in the diet (often dating back many years or even decades), as well as by some lack of vitamin D (both by inadequate ingestion and by inadequate exposure of the skin to sunlight) and by other hormonal and nutritional factors. Dietary surveys in selected places have shown that the calcium intake of older people is considerably lower than the Recommended Dietary Allowance (RDA) of 800 mg per day (Ten State Survey, 1968, 1970). In 1963 it was estimated that there were four million cases of severe osteoporosis among older people in the United States (HEW, 1965). Since this disease is more prevalent in women, it is possible that decreased levels of estrogens may be involved, although the calcium "drain" of pregnancy and lactation is also directly responsible. Studies in animals (Lutwak, 1974) have shown that the best example of the prevention of nutritional disability in old age is to ingest an adequate diet in earlier years, including especially sufficient protein, calcium, vitamin D, and fluoride. Furthermore, special attention to a high calcium intake should be made by those over 40 years of age.

Anemias are a particular problem for the aged, resulting from insufficiencies of iron, folic acid, and/or vitamin B^{12} (Clifford, 1971; Ho, 1968; Jacobs, 1971; Bose et al., 1970). A dietary deficiency of folic acid is probably due to the fact that dark-green leafy vegetables do not play a major role in the diet of the elderly. Furthermore, with aging there are changes in the gastric mucosa, achlorhydria, and possible diminution of the intrinsic factor which results in impairment of the absorption of vitamin B^{12}. Although anemias may be of mixed nutritional origin, pernicious anemia resulting from B^{12} deficiency is specifically a disease of old age (Clifford, 1971). Iron absorption is also impaired in the elderly and therefore iron-deficiency anemia is a common disorder (Evans, 1971; Aalberg et al., 1971; Jacobs, 1971).

A limited number of surveys has indicated that obesity is a problem with elderly people as well as with young adults (Rossman, 1971). This promotes a particular problem, because although obesity probably aggravates arthritis and other rheumatic diseases (Bender, 1971) and is undoubtedly a burden to the cardiovascular system, restriction of calories for weight reduction makes it difficult to provide the recommended amounts of the essential nutrients for this population. Moreover, malnutrition and undernutrition probably are responsible for many nonspecific symptoms observed in the elderly, such as mental confusion, chronic fatigue, listlessness, a general feeling of ill-health (Bender, 1971), and loss of appetite, eventually leading to even more pronounced malnutrition.

In 1975, 70% of the approximately one million persons in this country who succumbed to heart and blood vessel disease were 65 years or older. However, it should be remembered that atherosclerosis is a slowly progressive disease, initiated many years prior to the manifested event and resulting from many risk factors, among them a diet high in saturated fat. The aging process is accelerated by the onset of atherosclerosis. Elderly persons have difficulty with the absorption of fat and subsequent clearance of fat from blood and should be advised to eat low-fat diets which include a high proportion of polyunsaturated fat (Deuel, 1954). High-fiber diets have recently been reported to be helpful in controlling hypercholesterolemia, one of the risk factors in atherosclerosis and heart disease (Burkitt, 1976).

Often older people with "normal" metabolism become malnourished due to faulty eating patterns caused by difficulty in chewing because of poorly fitting dentures or lack of teeth. Meat and vegetables are avoided and carbohydrate foods which require little chewing are substituted. It is hoped that fluoride treatments of the teeth of the young or fluoridation of the water supply may overcome this nutritional difficulty for the elderly in the future. The presence of one part of fluoride in one million parts of water drastically decreases the frequency and severity of dental caries and is nontoxic (Nielsen et al., 1974).

Drug-Induced Malnutrition

Other nutritional problems may be related to the fact that many elderly people are taking various drugs or are on specialized diets for one or more chronic illnesses. All drugs affect the nutritional status of individuals. Aside from the secondary side effects, which include depressed appetite, nausea, vomiting, and diarrhea, drugs have direct effects on the metabolism of nutrients (Roe, 1976). Some drugs, for example, antibiotics, can produce changes in intestinal flora which are responsible for the synthesis of certain vitamins, in particular vitamin K and panthothenic acid. Destruction of intestinal bacteria may give rise to accelerated growth of fungi and to abnormal bacteria which may require excess amounts of folic acid and vitamin B^{12} for their growth and as a result deprive the host of these nutrients. Some drugs and medications may interfere with nutrient absorption. Iron supplements given to relieve anemia may inhibit the absorption of vitamin E. A resinous product, cholestyramine, given to reduce hypercholesterolemia, absorbs other important physiological substances with structures similar to cholesterol, for example, bile acids and vitamin D. The chronic use of alkalizers interferes with the absorption of many nutrients, including phosphate.

Other drugs, such as antimetabolites used in cancer therapy, interfere with the utilization of nutrients required for cell division and growth and thereby slow down or prevent abnormal growth of malignant tissues; at the same time the normal growth of healthy tissues is impaired. Some drugs result in the loss of nutrients through increased excretion. For instance, diuretics given for the control of hypertension prevent water retention but also enhance the excretion of potassium via the urine. Potassium has many functions in the body, among them the regulation of a normal heartbeat. Persons on diuretics should be encouraged to eat diets high in potassium.

In general, drug administration results in vitamin insufficiency. Even aspirin, if used continuously, leads to low vitamin C levels in leukocytes. Chronic alcohol ingestion results in reduced blood levels in vitamins B^1 and B^6 and folacin. Therefore, elderly people on drug therapy should be advised to take proper vitamin and mineral supplements when needed.

Recommendations for the Future: Nutritional Requirements

The recommended daily allowance of nutrients for healthy elderly persons is generally considered to be similar to that for healthy younger adults of the same sex, except for energy needs (RDA, 1974). Because older people lead less active, more sedentary lives, the energy needed for the day's activities, as well as energy required to maintain body processes, is reduced and therefore fewer calories from foods are required. Elderly persons still need protein, carbohydrate, fat, vitamins, minerals, and water. The question is: How different are the nutrient needs of older adults from younger adults? For example, is there a need for more protein to replace "worn out" tissues? Physical inactivity accelerates the loss of protein and, also, protein synthesis tends to be impaired in elderly persons. Although some investigators believe that evidence for increases in protein requirements with age are not conclusive (Irwin et al., 1971), others (Young et al., 1975) have suggested that some amino acid requirements may be higher in healthy elderly persons as compared with healthy young adults. Further exploration is needed to determine whether elderly adults require additional vitamin E to prevent the increasing number of oxidative reactions which accompany aging, more calcium to maintain a healthy skeleton and prevent osteoporosis, more vitamin C to protect against the stresses which accompany aging, and more iron to overcome any impairment in the absorption of this nutrient. However, no conclusive data are presently available to support recommendations for amounts of nutrients over and above those currently advised.

The elderly have been and are one of the most neglected population groups with respect to investigations of nutritional status and establishment of nutritional requirements. In the past this was primarily because of the limited numbers of people who lived longer than 65 years. This situation has changed dramatically in recent times.

Although in 1870 only 3% of the population (or 1.2 million) were 65 years or older, in 1976 the number of persons of 65 plus years in population has increased to 10.6% of the total, or 22.7 million persons. Due to a number of factors which have contributed and will continue to contribute to increased longevity, it is estimated that in the year 2000, the expected number of people over 65 years old will be approximately 30.6 million (Brotman, 1974). This may be an underestimate since ongoing research into causes of, and possibly improved therapy for the diseases which now claim the majority of the elderly will undoubtedly delay mortality and extend longevity.

However, merely extending longevity of an older population is not the primary goal of investigators. Rather it is the prime of life, the productive years, which needs to be extended. It is hoped the expected increase in this older segment of the population will result in the initiation of studies to elicit the required information to answer these important questions.

Foods of the Future

Foods of the future may help solve the nutritional problems of the elderly. First of all, fortification of foods to improve their nutrient content will help in combatting malnutrition. This is not a new concept. At present, bread flour is enriched with B vitamins and iron, milk is fortified with vitamins A and D, and salt is fortified with iodine. However, new breakthroughs in enrichment and fortification and new food technology have made possible the addition of other nutrients to foods, so that some presently widely used foods may in the future become complete nutritional sources. Furthermore, it may be possible to fortify basic foods, such as cereal products and other foods acceptable to the elderly, with selected nutrients so that all of the nutrient needs for selected population groups can be satisfied.

In addition, new foods are being developed. These are foods or food components put together in a new form or with a new composition designed to meet specific needs and problems. These may be "convenience" foods designed to save time and labor, "simulated" foods derived from various sources which can replace usual foods, or "synthetic" foods from "nonnatural" sources which can replace usual foods. For example, "simulated" foods are those made from textured vegetable proteins, which are becoming more and more useful in human nutrition. As prices steadily rise for those animal products which now provide most of our protein, and as animal protein becomes more scarce as a result of decreased grazing facilities, plant proteins will provide a higher proportion of our future protein intake. Although plant proteins do not have as high a biological value as animal proteins and they are low in several essential and nonessential amino acids (e.g., soy proteins are low in methionine and wheat and rice proteins are deficient in lysine), these missing amino acids can be added. Vegetable proteins can also be used to extend other sources of protein.

Besides being less expensive, plant proteins have other advantages, such as a longer storage life than animal protein, less flavor so that they can be mixed with other foods without changing their taste, and a form and texture easily digested by populations with dentures or digestive problems. Of course, pure vegetable proteins will be deficient in some of the other nutrients present in animal proteins, for example, iron and vitamin B^{12}. However, vegetable proteins are not intended as the sole dietary constituents; they are to be used in conjunction with other foods. Furthermore, vegetable proteins can be fortified with these missing nutrients if and when necessary.

Conclusions

Many of the diseases in which malnutrition presently plays a role will be eliminated, or at least decreased, by the year 2000. Judging from advances made in the treatments of cardiovascular disease, hypertension, diabetes, and osteoporosis, it is rational to believe that these diseases are likely to be much less common than they are today and as a result, healthy longevity will be increased. Fluoride treatments and other methods of proper dental care will insure against periodontal disease, maintain teeth, and enable the elderly to ingest and chew fibrous foods of all types, for example, fresh fruits, vegetables, and meats, all of which are necessary for good nutrition.

In the future, more exact information should be available as to the nutrient requirements of various age groups under all kinds of situations, such as exposure to differing climatic conditions and environmental factors, individual requirements resulting from genetic inheritance, and nutrient requirements which may have been altered by past episodes of disease conditions. These nutrient requirements could then be incorporated into diet plans which might take the form of prepackaged foods for the elderly with additions of specific nutrients suggested by the results of research findings. New flavors will have been originated that will make food more palatable to aging tastes. Wholesome, well-balanced snack foods will be available to provide calories as well as essential nutrients. It is estimated that adherence to these new, nutritionally optimal, prescribed diets may extend healthy longevity by 30 years; and healthy, productive centenarians should not be uncommon 25 years in the future.

References

Aalber, L., & Högdahl, A. Anemia and old age. *Gerontologia Clinica* (Basel), 1971, *31*, 12.

Bender, A. E. Nutrition of the elderly. *Royal Society of Health Journal*, 1971, *91*, 115–121.

Bose, S. D., Andrews, J., & Roberts, P. D. Hematological problems in a geriatric unit with special reference to anemia. *Gerontologia Clinica* (Basel), 1970, *12*, 339–346.

Brotman, H. B. Every tenth American? Statement prepared by United States Senate Special Committee on Aging, 1974.

Burkitt, D. The role of dietary fiber. *Nutrition Today*, 1976, *11*, 6.

Clifford, G. O. Hematological problems in the elderly. *Clinical Geriatrics*. Philadelphia; Lippincott, 1971, 253–266.

Couch, J. R., & Trammell, J. H. Effects of feeding low lysine starters and developers on growth, sexual maturity and subsequent performance of broiler breeder pullets. *British Poultry Science*, 1970, *11*, 489.

Deuel, J. J. Fat metabolism with special references to problems of aging. In *Symposium on Problems of Gerontology*, National Vitamin Foundation, Inc., 1954.

Evans, D. M. Hematological aspects of iron deficiency in the elderly. *Gerontologia Clinica* (Basel), 1971, *13*.

Harman, D. Free radical theory of aging. Effect of free radical reaction inhibitors on the mortality of LAF mice. *Journal of Gerontology*, 1968, *23*, 476.

Ho, R. Disorders of iron metabolism in geriatrics. *Geriatrics*, 1968, *23*, 79.

Irwin, M. I., & Hegsted, D. M. Protein requirements of man. *Journal of Nutrition*, 1971, *101*, 385.

Jacobs, P. Body iron loss in the geriatric patient. *Gerontologia Clinica* (Basel), 1970, *13*, 207.

Lutwak, L., Singer, F. R., & Urist, M. T. Current concepts of bone metabolism. *Annals of Internal Medicine*, 1974, *80*, 630–643.

McKay, C. M., Maynard, L. A., Sperling, G., & Barnes, L. L. Retarded growth, life span ultimate body size and changes in the albino rat after feeding diets restricted in calories. *Journal of Nutrition*, 1939, *18*, 1.

Medvedev, Zh. A. *Biological Aspects of Aging*, N. W. Shock, (Ed.). New York: Columbia University Press, 1960.

Nielsen, G. H., & Sandstead, H. H. Are nickel, vanadium, silicon, fluorine and tin essential to man? A review. *American Journal of Clinical Nutrition*, 1974, *27*, 518.

Ram, J. Sri. Aging and immunologic phenomena. A review. *Journal of Gerontology*, 1967, *22*, 92.

Recommended dietary allowance. National Academy of Sciences, 8th Edition, 1974.

Roe, D. *Drug Induced Nutritional Deficiencies*. Westport, Connecticut: Avi Press, 1967.

Ross, M. G. *Diet and Bodily Constitution*. New York: Little, Brown, Ciba Foundation Study Group, 1964, *17*, 90.

Rossman, I., The anatomy of aging. In *Clinical Geriatrics*, Philadelphia: Lippincott, 1971.

Singsen, E. P., Nagel, J., Patrick. S. G., & Matterson, L. D. The effect of lysine deficiency on growth characteristics, age at sexual maturity, and reproductive performance of meat-type pullets. *Poultry Science*, 1965, *44*, 1467.

Tappel, A. L., Will anti-oxidants slow aging process? *Geriatrics*, 1968, *23*, 97.

Tappel, A. L. Free radical peroxidation of lipids. *Annals of New York Academy of Science*, 1972, *203*, 12–27.

Ten State Nutrition Survey (1968–1970). Preliminary Report to the Congress, Atlanta, Ga., United States Department HEW, Center for Disease Control, 1971.

United States Department of HEW Information Office, National Institute of Arthritis and Metabolic Diseases, Bethseda, Md. Public

Health Service Publication N 1217, Health Information Series N. 118, January, 1965.

Wulff, V. J., Quastler, H., & Sherman, F. G. Hypothesis concerning RNA metabolism and aging. *Proceedings of National Academy of Science*, 1962, *48*, 1373.

Young, V., & Scrimshaw, N. Total body protein synthesis in relation to protein requirements of various ages. *Nature*, 1975, *253*, 192.

PART TWO
SOCIETAL RESPONSE:
Psychological Perspectives

COMMENTARY

Nutritional needs of the body have a parallel in nutritional needs of the mind as pointed out by Asenath LaRue and Lissy Jarvik who debunk the myth of intellectual decline as an inevitable concomitant of advancing chronological age. Marjorie Fiske too emphasizes that the elderly are not a homogeneous group. Her attack on the monolithic "aged" opens the path to Martin Grotjahn's advocacy of group therapy as a means for engendering group communication, individual motivation, and acceptance of life as it has been lived and death as it must come. And in the future it may come as foreseen in Carl Eisdorfer's at times chilling vista of societal response to stereotyped aging. There are, unfortunately, some similarities between his futuristic death houses and far too many present day nursing homes. Although institutional settings are likely to persist into the 21st century, many of their negative features may not, and Bernice Neugarten foresees educational programs designed to ascertain the "best death" for each individual. And even today, we have Roslyn Lindheim, one of the few architects who stresses designs for living and not designs for dying. In line with the spirit of continued life, growth, and activity in old age, Howard McClusky, a pioneer in the world of adult education, envisions learning for living. He proposes a lifetime education process, beginning with earlier preparation for the demands of the later years, workers' sabbaticals, continuing education for adults, and education for second and possibly third careers. Among the latter may well be careers in politics. However, George Maddox, one of our leading social gerontologists, feels that a gerontocracy is an unlikely development for the 21st century and that senior power will not be the wave of the future.

6

AGING AND INTELLECTUAL FUNCTIONING:
Great Expectations?

ASENATH LaRUE and LISSY F. JARVIK

Introduction

What will the intellectual status of older persons be in the 21st century? Current data indicate that those over 65 years of age are likely to be healthier, wealthier, and perhaps somewhat wiser in the future than they are today. In this chapter, we discuss some of the bases for a positive outlook regarding intelligence and aging and some factors that limit optimistic projections. Speculations regarding the future roles of those who study aging and the intellect will be presented in a concluding section.

Rationale for Positive Projections

The prediction of better intellectual functioning among the old of the future, compared to the old of the present, is based upon the fact that improvements are expected in several variables with which intelligence has traditionally been correlated: most notably, health status and education. Several contributors to this volume have commented on the expected increases in these correlates (e.g., Comfort, Eisdorfer, Maddox, and McClusky) and hence, the bases for these expectations will be mentioned only briefly here.

Improved health status, albeit to a moderate degree, can be expected if appropriate medical and social action is taken in the coming years. Current federal programs (i.e., Medicare/Medicaid) have made medical assistance more accessible to older persons than before. If such programs can keep pace with predicted increases in the number of elderly persons, the average health status of the future aged is likely to exceed that of today. Even more importantly, the probable implementation of some form of national health insurance in the near future will enable adults to maintain their health to a more adequate degree before old age than is the custom now. Some benefit to health status may also accrue from recent improvements in pension plans (e.g., the Employee Retirement Income Security Act of 1974), although it is too soon to tell what the extent of participation in such plans will be or what proportion of the funds accrued in this manner will be spent on health services. Finally, 20 or more years is not too short a time span in which to expect some improvement in the prevention and treatment of those diseases which have disproportionate effects upon the elderly, such as stroke. Even today, the most frequent single cause of stroke, hypertension, is treatable, and yet a considerable proportion of hypertensives fail to adhere to recommended medical regimens, including use of the antihypertensive drugs and lifestyle changes that would control their disease. Indeed, lifestyle seems to be a major variable in the diseases to which a disproportionately high number of the aged are prone, and changes in lifestyle seem to be the most difficult to effect (e.g., elimination of obesity, smoking, and alcoholism, to name the most common detrimental influences on the health of the aged). Health education clearly has a vital role to play here.

As for general educational status, there are several ways in which the attainment of older persons in the 21st century can be expected to exceed current levels. At present, 42% of the elderly have had eight or fewer years of initial, formal education (Harris & associates, 1975); by 1990, however, the average older person can be expected to have at least a high school degree (Neugarten, 1975). In addition, as McClusky's chapter illustrates, adult education classes are likely to be more numerous and comprehensive in the years to come; greater participation in such classes should be expected with improvements in health among older persons (Goodnow, 1975). Finally, the elderly of the future are likely to lead more complex and active lives and they will thereby encounter many more informal educational experiences in the occupational, physical, and social realms (e.g., De Carlo, 1971).

Assuming for the moment that these improvements occur, we can turn to an examination of current data relating health status, education, and intellectual functioning in older persons. Although the link between health and mental performance has long been recognized (e.g., Birren,

Butler, Greenhouse, Sokoloff, & Yarrow, 1963), recent reviews have underscored the strength of the relationship between these variables. Siegler (1975) examined the results of eight major longitudinal studies and observed: ". . . it appears that physical health is important for, not only survival, but also for the maintenance of cognitive abilities" (p. 179). Abrahams (1976) came to a similar conclusion on the basis of his review of the literature: "Regardless of the debate concerning the nature and extent of age-associated alterations in intellectual functioning, health status has been shown to influence scores on both verbal and non-verbal measures" (p. 65).

In view of the general support that the health/intellect relation has received, it is instructive to consider studies which have found only weak correlations between these variables. Certain of the negative findings can be explained in statistical and methodological terms. Botwinick and Birren (1963) compared the performance of two groups of elderly men on WAIS subscales and other cognitive measures; one group consisted of men without health difficulties and the other included individuals with mild, asymptomatic problems. Although the disease-free group typically exceeded the other in performance, significant differences were observed on only six of 23 measures. In this case, nonsignificance appears to have resulted from restriction of range on the health dimension. Unless properly identified, such restricted variation could lead not only to an underestimation of the importance of health in the absolute sense, but also to an overestimation of the significance of other variables, such as chronological age (Abrahams, 1976; Botwinick & Arenberg, 1976). It is only through the study of numerous health contrasts that researchers can discover what constitutes an important health variation vis-à-vis intelligence and other variables.

Not all negative findings are attributable to factors of sampling and design, however. Some measures of intelligence are more sensitive to health differences than others, and different aspects of health relate to the same measure in divergent ways. Jarvik and Cohen (1973) concluded that speeded performance was more strongly correlated with certain specific indices of biological state than with general health status. Hence, performance on a speeded psychomotor task (i.e., tapping) has consistently failed to differentiate decedents from survivors in a 20-year longitudinal study of aging twins (e.g., Jarvik & Blum, 1971; Jarvik & Falek, 1963), but significant correlations have been observed between reaction time and certain indices of cardiovascular disease (e.g., Abrahams & Birren, 1973; Spieth, 1964). By contrast, decline in performance on some WAIS verbal subtests is strongly related to five-year mortality in elderly subjects (Birren, 1968; Jarvik & Blum, 1971; Jarvik & Falek, 1963) and only weakly associated with earlier, nonchronic fluctuations in physical status. These observations illustrate the need to compare profiles of physical and mental functioning rather than point estimates of health and intellect in general.

A final issue with regard to health/intellect correspondences concerns the lack of studies relating health status to performance on laboratory tests of learning and cognition. Most experimental studies fail to report the physical status of their elderly subjects (Abrahams, Hoyer, Elias, & Bradigan, 1975); in cases in which such information is available, participation is typically limited to healthy persons (e.g., Robertson-Tchabo & Arenberg, 1976). Only a few investigations have examined adults' performance on Piagetian tests of cognition (see Papalia & Bielby, 1974, for a review), and adequate health information has been lacking in most of these studies to date. There is evidence, however, that basic Piagetian concepts, such as conservation, are greatly impaired in elderly patients with organic brain syndrome. Similar findings regarding the effects of this syndrome have been reported with standardized intelligence measures (e.g., Savage, Britton, Bolton, & Hall, 1973). Both sets of results underscore the need to separate normal and pathological aging.

In summarizing the present relation between health status and intellectual functioning among the aged, it is important to note that the correspondence is complex and relevant data are available for only certain types of mental performance. However, the relation between these two classes of variables is positive and reasonably strong. No one has reported that healthy old people are less mentally able than unhealthy ones!

Education has been related to intellectual functioning more frequently than health, and numerous reviews attest to the significance of this relationship for the understanding of adult behavior and aging (e.g., Baltes & Labouvie, 1973; Schaie, 1974). Differences in initial educational level are currently predictive not only of mean differences in adult mental functioning (e.g., Birren & Morrison, 1961) but also of differential rates of intellectual change. Data from a longitudinal study of aging twins (Blum & Jarvik, 1974) indicated that those who had some initial secondary school education declined at a slower rate late in life than those whose initial education had terminated at the primary school level. With regard to younger age ranges,

Honzik and MacFarlane (1973) reported that highly educated persons were more likely to gain in IQ from 18 to 40 years than those who were less well educated.

Continuing education, both formal and informal, also has important effects on adult mental functioning. Not surprisingly, adults whose occupations require high levels of intellectual activity typically score higher on a variety of measures than those in less intellectually demanding jobs (e.g., Hawley & Kelley, Note 1; Vernon, 1947). Some support for a relation between informal educational activity (i.e., intellectual, physical, and social stimulation) and mental functioning is also available. De Carlo (1971) rated aging twins on dimensions of physical, mental, and social activity; high activity was associated with high scores on an index of successful aging which included cognitive components. Belbin and Belbin (1969) reported that older adults with "mentally-active" spare-time interests were more likely to be successful in a vocational training program than adults who were lacking in such interests. Finally, Honzik and MacFarlane (1973) noted that 40-year-olds with high IQs were likely to have high aspiration levels, to value intellectual and cognitive matters, and to be concerned with philosophical problems.

Although there does seem to be a relation between intelligence and continued activity, two recent studies illustrate the need to consider activity in conjunction with health variables. Troll, Saltz, and Dunin-Markiewicz (1976) conducted a longitudinal follow-up of elderly persons who had been active in a foster grandparent program. Performance on selected WAIS subscales was generally found to be stable over the seven-year period; for participants with declining health, however, a significant drop in intellectual performance was observed. It appears, therefore, that continued involvement and stimulation cannot totally override the negative effects of poor health among older persons. Kleban, Lawton, Brody, and Moss (1976) studied elderly institutionalized women with moderate to severe organic brain syndrome over a two-year period. Cognitive functioning was periodically assessed and weekly ratings were obtained regarding activity and interest in work and social relations. Changes in the activity measures were found to be unrelated to changes in cognitive abilities. This study indicates that activity and intelligence may be related in divergent ways among members of different health groups.

A final set of data on educational effects is provided by recent studies in which an attempt has been made to improve mental performance in elderly subjects through specific, short-term training. To date, some significant effects (e.g., Hornblum & Overton, 1976; Hultsch, 1971), some nonsignificant effects (e.g., Hoyer, Labouvie, & Baltes, 1973), and some effects differing from predictions (e.g., Labouvie-Vief & Gonda, 1976) have been obtained. The data base of training studies is still fairly small and several suggestions for improvements in this approach can be made; however, such studies generally lend support to the concept of intellectual plasticity in older persons.

Many of the same summary comments can be made regarding the relation between education and intellectual functioning as between health and mental performance in the later years. We know less than we would like to know, especially about specific mechanisms; but the existence of a correspondence between intelligence and education, both formal and informal, is undeniable among the aged of today.

We have now listed some reasons for our hope that the health and education of older persons in the 21st century will exceed that of today and have asserted our belief that these variables are related in important ways to the mental functioning of older persons at the present time. It would be desirable to be able to conclude that mental functioning of the elderly in the future will be greatly and significantly improved. However, a more moderate expectancy is in order, as the following considerations indicate.

Limitations on Optimistic Predictions and Some Unanswered Questions

Predictions about aging and mental functioning in the future must be based, of course, on some model of intellectual development (Baltes & Labouvie, 1973; Overton & Reese, 1973; Schaie, 1973). In projecting greater mental performance among the aged of the 21st century, we are adopting for expediency a linear causality model with physical status, education, and activity as antecedents and intellectual functioning as the consequent. This model is certainly inadequate (cf. Jarvik, 1975), and even if it were not, very few of our present data are of the type to permit inference of antecedent–consequent relations. The healthier, better educated adults of the future will undoubtedly alter the course of their own aging in ways that are difficult to anticipate today. Moreover, altered health and educational environments will interact with genetic factors to produce patterns of aging which are as yet unexpressed. Nevertheless, the present predictions may prove to be reasonably accurate if (a) future correlations between health, education, and intellectual functioning are similar to those of today and (b) current and future methods of intellectual assessment are sufficiently related. The first of these conditions is likely to be met for direction of association, if not for magnitude. Perhaps the second condition will also hold, even though there is certainly a need for improvement in assessment batteries for adults (e.g., Schaie, Note 2).

There is a second source of limitations on optimistic projections. That is, we have been assuming that it is in some way meaningful to generalize about intellectual functioning some 20 years from now. Yet, one of the major findings of all longitudinal studies is that, for a given chronological age span, some individuals will be experiencing declining mental functioning, some will be stable, and others will be continuing to increase in tested intelligence. A study of aging twins indicated that these individual differences are present to some degree even for persons with identical genetic makeup and relatively similar life histories (e.g., Blum & Jarvik, 1971). The existence of such variability need not invalidate predictive attempts but it certainly reduces one's confidence in generalized projections.

Our predictions for older persons have suffered so far from another aspect of what Eisdorfer has called "conglomerate definition." Specifically, we have made no distinction between the future intellectual functioning of those who will be very old (i.e., 75 years or more) from those who will be old to a lesser degree (cf. Neugarten, 1975). Studies using sequential designs typically find that cohort differences account for a smaller proportion of intellectual variance at advanced ages than at earlier points in adulthood (e.g., Schaie, Labouvie, & Buech, 1973). Similarly, intellectual performance and distance-from-death are also less clearly related among the very old as opposed to the merely old (Jarvik & Blum, 1971; Riegel & Riegel, 1972). We do not know the extent to which future improvements in health and education will alter this picture, but it is clear that further study of the genetic and biological bases of aging is crucial for our understanding of persons who are very old.

A final shadow on our optimism about future intellectual aging is that we cannot anticipate what the response of society as a whole will be to intellectual advances among older persons. As McClusky indicates, society does not as yet accept the fact that older persons can learn, nor does it endorse their right to further education. Will this attitude change in 20-odd years? The intellectual advances of older persons, whatever they may be, will inevitably be assessed relative to the mental capabilities of their younger contemporaries. We can hope, of course, that the knowledge and abilities of future old persons will rank favorably with those of future young persons (Schaie, 1974).

In summary, a consideration of assumptions and unanswered questions necessitates a moderate statement of expectations: The future intellectual functioning of older persons will exceed that of today to an unknown degree; this improvement with successive decades will not be shared by all old persons; and the advances may go unnoticed by other segments of society.

Toward the Study of Aging and Intelligence in the Future

It is difficult to anticipate the questions which will be asked about intelligence by gerontologists in the 21st century. With regard to the next few years, however, several directions for research can be proposed.

It is to be hoped that studies in the near future will take a more psychobiological approach to the topic of intellect and aging than has previously been the case (Jarvik, 1975; Jarvik & Cohen, 1973). This approach could take several forms, from simple to complex. It would be helpful, of course, if more investigators included health status as a variable in their designs (Abrahams, 1976; Abrahams et al., 1975). At the very least, adequate description of samples on health-status dimensions would enable reviewers to determine whether contradictions in the literature might be due to differences in participants' physical status. An example of the utility of such information was provided by Siegler (1975) in her recent review of data pertaining to the terminal drop hypothesis. After examining the results of several longitudinal studies and a variety of cross-sectional reports, she concluded that health is an important factor in determining the relation between cognitive performance and distance from death; specifically, significant relations are more likely to be found among relatively healthy samples than among samples in which organic brain dysfunction is prevalent (p. 180).

Such a global version of the psychobiological approach must be complemented by research concerning the specific mechanisms which underlie health and mental-functioning relations. Hypertension, for example, has been linked with cognitive decline (Wilkie & Eisdorfer,

1973) and chromosome loss with senile dementia (Jarvik, Altshuler, Kato, & Blumner, 1971; Nielsen, 1968). A relationship has also been demonstrated between chromosome loss and poor performance on certain cognitive tasks (Jarvik, 1973), and recent data indicate a possible association between chromosome loss and immune changes (Matsuyama, Cohen, & Jarvik, in preparation), and between immune levels and cognitive performance (Cohen, Matsuyama, & Jarvik, 1976).

Studies which attempt to manipulate intellectual performance are also likely to be more numerous in the near future. The combined efforts of specialists in gerontology, learning, and cognition will be required to achieve maximum productivity from this approach, however. Studies to date have convincingly shown that the performance of the elderly can be improved with practice and experience, but the extent of improvement is at times unrelated to specific treatment conditions (e.g., Hoyer et al., 1973). Similarly, the persistence and generalization of training effects does not always appear to be related to the structure and specificity of training procedures (e.g., Labouvie-Vief & Gonda, 1976).

This confusing pattern of training effects is reminiscent of the outcomes of studies in the early 1960s which attempted to manipulate children's conservation skills. These early studies either failed to obtain significant effects of training or failed to demonstrate generalization to related tasks (see Brainerd & Allen, 1971, for a review). By contrast, more recent research on conservation has produced both sizeable training and generalization effects (e.g., Brainerd, 1974; Gelman, 1969). The relative success of the latter studies appears to have resulted from several factors: (a) a better understanding of the rules that children normally used to solve conservation tasks, (b) consideration of the manner in which initial performance levels interact with subsequent training, and (c) greater articulation of the limits of generalization, i.e., specification of those tasks for which generalization should and should not be anticipated.

Parallel advances in the cognitive training of older persons may be accomplished by another decade of research. Studies which compare several different subgroups of subjects (e.g., of different ages, health status, or educational levels) are likely to be most useful (Gollin, 1965). Similarly, the inclusion of several different generalization tasks could aid in the determination of the limits of effectiveness of a given training program (cf. Brainerd, 1974). Finally, it would be interesting if generalization tasks were to include some practical skills from the occupational or personal–legal realms. The resulting data would provide information about the external validity of laboratory tasks and experimental–manipulative techniques.

Gerontologists in the future will also be engaged in the interpretation of results from descriptive longitudinal and sequential studies. In the past, these data-collection strategies have permitted the isolation of intellectual-aging functions that are predictive of mortality. Repeated assessment of the senescent twins, for example, has resulted in an empirically defined concept of "critical loss" which has been shown to be a relatively accurate predictor of mortality within a five-year interval after the last test occasion (e.g., Jarvik & Blum, 1971; Jarvik & Falek, 1963). In the future, it may be possible to define similar patterns of changes within a battery of intellectual and personal-social variables that will be predictive of individuals' reactions to other significant life-cycle events such as retirement or vocational retraining. Longitudinal and sequential studies will also be needed to disentangle the complex interactions among physical, educational, and lifestyle determinants of intellectual functioning per se.

Concluding speculations are concerned with a possible extended role for future gerontologists with an interest in intellectual functioning. In lieu of definitive statements about the intellectual competence of older persons, industries will continue to make retirement and retraining decisions on the basis of economic conditions and college curricula will expand and contract in pursuit of the adult education market. It would be desirable to assess the cognitive impact of a large number of these natural experiments. To be permitted to do so, gerontologists must convince individuals, institutions, and society as a whole of the value of their knowledge and services.

References

Abrahams, J. P. Health status as a variable in aging research. *Experimental Aging Research*, 1976, *2*, 63–71.

Abrahams, J. P., & Birren, J. E. Reaction time as a function of age and behavioral predisposition to coronary heart disease. *Journal of Gerontology*, 1973, *28*, 471–478.

Abrahams, J. P., Hoyer, W. J., Elias, M. F., & Bradigan, B. Gerontological research published in the *Journal of Gerontology* 1963–1974: Perspectives and progress. *Journal of Gerontology*, 1975, *30*, 668–673.

Baltes, P. B., & Labouvie, G. V. Adult development of intellectual performance: Description, explanation, and modification. In C. Eisdorfer and M. P. Lawton (Eds.), *The Psychology of Adult Development and Aging*. Washington, D. C.: American Psychological Association, 1973.

Birren, J. E. Increment and decrement in the intellectual status of the aged. *Psychiatric Research Reports*, 1968, *23*, 207–214.

Birren, J. E., Butler, R. N., Greenhouse, S. W., Sokoloff, L., & Yarrow, M. (Eds.) *Human Aging: A Biological and Behavioral Study*. Washington, D. C.: United States Government Printing Office, 1963.

Birren, J. E., & Morrison, D. E. Analysis of the WAIS subtests in relation to age and education. *Journal of Gerontology*, 1961, *16*, 363–369.

Belbin, E., & Belbin, R. M. Selecting and training adults for new work. In A. T. Welford (Ed.), *Decision Making and Age*. New York: Karger, 1969.

Blum, J. E., & Jarvik, L. F. Intellectual performance of octogenarians as a function of education and initial ability. *Human Development*, 1974, *17*, 364–375.

Botwinick, J., & Arenberg, D. Disparate time spans in sequential studies of aging. *Experimental Aging Research*, 1976, *2*, 55–61.

Botwinick, J., & Birren, J. E. Cognitive processes: Mental abilities and psychomotor responses in healthy aged men. In J. E. Birren, R. N. Butler, S. W. Greenhouse, L. Sokoloff, & M. Yarrow (Eds.), *Human Aging: A Biological and Behavioral Study*. Washington, D. C.: United States Government Printing Office, 1963.

Brainerd, C. J. Training and transfer of transitivity, conservation, and class inclusion of length. *Child Development*, 1974, *45*, 324–334.

Brainerd, C. J. & Allen, T. W. Experimental inductions of conservation of "first-order" quantitative invariants. *Psychological Bulletin*, 1971, *75*, 128–144.

Cohen, D., Matsuyama, S. S., & Jarvik, L. F. Immunoglobulin levels and intellectual functioning in the aged. *Experimental Aging Research*, 1976, *2*, 345–348.

DeCarlo, T. Recreation patterns and successful aging: A twin study. Unpublished doctoral dissertation. Columbia University, 1971.

Gelman, R. Conservation acquisition: A problem of learning to attend to relevant attributes. *Journal of Experimental Child Psychology*, 1969, *7*, 167–187.

Gollin, E. S. A developmental approach to learning and cognition. In L. P. Lipsitt, & C. C Spiker (Eds.), *Advances in Child Development and Behavior* (Vol. 2). New York: Academic Press, 1965.

Goodnow, B. A. Limiting factors in reducing participation in older adult learning opportunities. *The Gerontologist*, 1975, *15*, 418–422.

Harris, L., and associates. *The Myth and Reality of Aging in America*. National Council on Aging, Washington, D. C., 1975.

Honzik, M. P., & Macfarlane, J. W. Personality development and intellectual functioning from 21 months to 40 years. In L. F. Jarvik, C. Eisdorfer, & J. E. Blum (Eds.), *Intellectual Functioning in Adults*. New York: Springer, 1973.

Hornblum, J. N., & Overton, W. F. Area and volume conservation among the elderly: Assessment and training. *Developmental Psychology*, 1976, *12*, 68–74.

Hoyer, W. J., Labouvie, G. V., & Baltes, P. B. Modification of response speed deficits and intellectual performance in the elderly. *Human Development*, 1973, *16*, 233–242.

Hultsch, D. Adult age differences in free classification and free recall. *Developmental Psychology*, 1971, *4*, 338–342.

Jarvik, L. F. Memory loss and its possible relationship to chromosome changes. In C. Eisdorfer and W. E Fann (Eds.), *Psychopharmacology and Aging*. New York: Plenum Press, 1973.

Jarvik, L. F. Thoughts on the psychobiology of aging. *American Psychologist*, 1975, *30*, 576–583.

Jarvik, L. F., Altshuler, K. Z., Kato, T., & Blumner, B. Organic brain syndrome and chromosome loss in aged twins. *Diseases of the Nervous System*, 1971, *32*, 159–170.

Jarvik, L. F., & Blum, J. E. Cognitive declines as predictors of mortality in discordant twin pairs: A twenty-year longitudinal study of aging. In E. Palmore, & F. C. Jeffers (Eds.), *Prediction of Life Span*. Lexington, Mass.: Heath Lexington, 1971.

Jarvik, L. F., & Cohen, D. A biobehavioral approach to intellectual changes with aging. In C. Eisdorfer, & M. P. Lawton (Eds.), *The Psychology of Adult Development and Aging*. American Psychological Association, Washington, D. C, 1973.

Jarvik, L. F., & Falek, A. Intellectual stability and survival in the aged. *Journal of Gerontology*, 1963, *18*, 173–176.

Kleban, M. H., Lawton, M. P., Brody, E. M., & Moss, M. Behavioral observations of mentally impaired aged: Those who decline and those who do not. *Journal of Gerontology*, 1976, *31*, 333–339.

Labouvie-Vief, G., & Gonda, J. N. Cognitive strategy training and intellectual performance in the elderly. *Journal of Gerontology*, 1976, *31*, 327–332.

Nielsen, J. Chromosomes in senile dementia. *British Journal of Psychiatry*, 1968, *115*, 303–309.

Neugarten, B. The future and the young-old. *The Gerontologist*, 1975, *15*, 4–9.

Overton, W. F., & Reese, H. W. Models of development: Methodological implications. In J. R. Nesselroade, & H. W. Reese (Eds.), *Lifespan Development Psychology: Methodological Issues*. New York: Academic Press, 1973.

Papalia, D. E., & Bielby, D. Cognitive functioning in middle- and old-age adults. *Human Development*, 1974, *17*, 424—443.

Riegel, K. F., & Riegel, R. M. Development, drop, and death. *Developmental Psychology*, 1972, *6*, 306–319.

Robertson-Tchabo, E. A., & Arenberg, D. Age differences in cognition in healthy educated men: A factor analysis of experimental measures. _Experimental Aging Research_, 1976, _2_, 75–79.

Savage, R. D., Britton, P. C., Bolton, N., & Hall, E. H. _Intellectual Functioning in the Aged_. London: Methuen, 1973.

Schaie, K. W. Methodological problems in descriptive developmental research on adulthood and aging. In J. R. Nesselroade, & H. W. Reese (Eds.), _Life-span Developmental Psychology:Methodological Issues_. New York: Academic Press, 1973.

Schaie, K. W. Translations in gerontology—Lab to life: Intellectual functioning. _American Psychologist_, 1974, _29_, 802–807.

Schaie, K. W., Labouvie, G. V., & Buech, B. U. Generational cohort-specific differences in adult cognitive functioning: A fourteen-year study of independent samples. _Developmental Psychology_, 1973, _9_, 151–166.

Siegler, I. C. The terminal drop hypothesis: Fact or artifact? _Experimental Aging Research_, 1975, _1_, 169–185.

Spieth, W. Cardiovascular health status, age and psychological performance. _Journal of Gerontology_, 1964, _19_, 277–284.

Troll, L. E., Saltz, R., & Dunin-Markiewicz, A. A seven-year follow-up of intelligence test scores of foster grandparents. _Journal of Gerontology_, 1976, _31_, 583–585.

Vernon, P. E. The variation of intelligence with occupation, age, and locality. _British Journal of Psychology_, 1947, _1_, 52–63.

Wilkie, F. L., & Eisdorfer, C. Systemic disease and behavioral correlates. In L. F. Jarvik, C. Eisdorfer, & J. E. Blum (Eds.), _Intellectual Functioning in Adults_. New York: Springer, 1973.

Reference Notes

1. Hawley, I., & Kelley, F. J. Formal operations among adults as a function of age, education, and fluid and crystallized intelligence. Paper presented at the meeting of the Gerontology Society, Miami, 1973.

2. Schaie, K. W. Competence and intelligence. Paper presented at the annual meeting of the Western Psychological Association, Los Angeles, 1976.

7

THE REALITY OF PSYCHOLOGICAL CHANGE

MARJORIE FISKE

Introduction

Although questions and data from epidemiological and biological perspectives are of critical importance for policy and planning in both the public and the private sectors, ranging from medical to social and economic planning, the fact remains that even with no major population shifts whatsoever we can expect to face serious problems as we enter the 21st century, unless we can locate and identify those points where the gaps between the needs of the individual and the prevailing value systems, both institutional and general, are the greatest!

This seems a legitimate conclusion from an examination of the current dilemmas and frustrations of persons who will be, to utilize Bernice Neugarten's important distinctions, "young-old" and "old-old" in the year 2000.

Whether these segments of the population increase or decrease in terms of secular trends, present medical and actuarial knowledge makes it reasonable to assume that a high proportion of those who are now in these cohorts will survive to the turn of the century.

In many sectors the lacunae between individual needs, on the one hand, and social institutions and the prevailing norms, on the other, seem to be widening and threaten to produce not only a great waste of social resources but a large population at risk from both mental health and physical health perspectives. For the growing cohorts of people now in relatively good health, facing an unprecedented 15 to 30 years of postparental and retirement periods, the times are seriously out of joint.

The vast "middle majority" of such people are rather surprised to find themselves confronting these lengthy and bleakly unfilled prospective years; and they are neither equipped nor motivated to do much of anything about it themselves. This is so, in part, because the educational systems and the normative expectations by which they have been conditioned early in life have failed to take into account theoretical and practical issues relating to this period of the adult life course. Outmoded concepts still prevail in our educational institutions, for the most part, so there is as yet little possibility of change via a potentially more enlightened view on the part of the adolescent and young adult children of cohorts with which we are concerned. Although the burgeoning thrust of educational opportunities for senior citizens may help, until it becomes a part of a lifelong process it will be a mere palliative.

In saying that those cohorts which will be in their 60s, 70s, and 80s at the beginning of the 21st century are not likely to do much about these matters themselves, I am, of course, agreeing with George Maddox and others who have considered the issues bearing on a potential political gerontocracy. The basis for my pessimism in regard to what these cohorts are going to do about their personal destinies, and what role models they will establish for future cohorts confronting these later life stages, is an intensive study of persons facing the normative transitions of the adult life course. The data come from the first phase of a longitudinal study being conducted by the Human Development Program at the University of California, San Francisco (Lowenthal, Thurnher, Chiriboga, & associates, 1975).

Although we are also studying younger adults, I shall report here primarily on the predicaments and crises of middle-aged people who will be in their late 70s and early 80s in the 21st century and those who, facing imminent retirement now, will then be in their 90s. This will be followed by a description of the experienced stresses by these men and women, and the stance toward stress reported by them.

I would also like briefly to sketch out some of the major psychosocial problems confronting people who were in or approaching the postparental and retirement stages at the time of our initial contact with them (1970–1971), and what we see as implications for the future. Further documentation is available in a recently completed book (Lowenthal et al., 1975). From a broad array of important psychosocial issues, I shall touch upon three or four having to do with perceptions of stress, of pending transitions, of stance toward the future, and of some of the personal and social resources and impediments which help or hinder the efforts of this cohort to cope with the inevitable life-course changes that accompany the aging process. These personal problems are compounded, of course, by the unprecedented acceleration of economic, environmental, and cultural changes in the world around them.

I shall continue with a note on buffers against stress and psychological crises and observations about life-course "careers" in work, family, and leisure spheres, and I shall conclude with some projections of the implications of these trends for the 21st century. It should be noted that in the life stages we are studying, sex differences are generally of higher magnitude than stage differences and prevail in nearly all areas. In fact, the life-course trajectories—and in turn the needs, goals, and problems—of men and women do not parallel each other but at points threaten a potential collision course.

Sociopolitical Stance

The groups studied were relatively small but carefully drawn samples from the middle and lower class, largely Caucasian population of a large metropolitan area. The subjects in our "four stages of life" resided in an unusually stable and homogeneous district of small, rather uniform homes. The youngest sample (high school seniors) was a random one drawn from the neighborhood high school's records, a school which was selected for its socioeconomic and ethnic homogeneity. Because this was an intensive research undertaking we could not confound it with too many variables. The middle-aged people facing the empty nest phase were also drawn from the school records. The newly-wed sample was drawn from vital statistics, randomly selected from persons living in the same area, while the preretirement group was "snow-balled" from these samples, having also lived for a considerable time in the same area.

They seemed to be, in the psychosocial issues with which we are concerned, representative of their life stages, class, and ethnic counterparts elsewhere in the country. That they were not likely to have much political impact on issues vital to them now and in the 21st century is a conclusion based on their segmented concern with social and political issues, concern which was limited almost exclusively to problems which impinged on them personally, such as their economic welfare and safety on the streets. The in-depth interviewing on questions dealing with local, national, and international issues revealed a profoundly anomic stance toward the efficacy of any conceivable role in relation to such issues for people like themselves, even at the community level.

Stress Perceptions and Stance of Men

This study was at the outset designed, in part, to test the rather optimistic self-actualization concepts of such theorists as Allport (1955), Maslow (1954), Erikson (1974, 1975), Bühler (1968), and Fromm (1976), whose studies were largely based on samples of talented and privileged individuals, including perhaps a measure of introspection about their talented and privileged selves. Our sample, in contrast, has been in that increasing segment of the population which has begun to assimilate some of the values of the upper middle class but remains primarily job (security) and family oriented. The pervasiveness of occupational and familial concerns became apparent when we inspected the nature of what they considered stressful when they adopted a life-course perspective, both retrospective and prospective.

In this study, the number of life-course events and circumstances perceived as stressful declined across the adult life course. There was a sharp demarcation between newlyweds and the middle-aged; there were only slight differences between the middle-aged confronting the postparental stage and those facing imminent retirement (the average age difference between these two older groups was 10 years).

Work-related problems were critical for the middle-aged men, mainly having to do with the pressures of providing sufficient income to maintain a comfortable lifestyle through the retirement period. In view of the fact that the majority were firmly entrenched in the probable security of civil service and related bureaucracies (indeed, many had selected such work primarily because of its security), and above all in view of the remoteness of their retirement (10 to 15 years), it is likely that much of this preoccupation and anxiety was attributable to a combination of job frustration and economic and political factors beyond their control. Incidentally, the men at middle-age and pre-retirement, unlike younger men and unlike women in all four stages, showed little sign of continuing to suffer from the effects of any early deprivation (such as loss of a parent). However, having grown up during the Great Depression, they were almost obsessed with financial security.

The mixture of strain and boredom that we observed

in the middle-aged men struck us as a threat to their mental health in succeeding years. To the extent that their economic fears were, or were to become, realistic, they would also appear to constitute a potentially susceptible target group for any charismatic political leaders who might arise in the next 15 or 20 years—particularly in view of their concern with law and order—those from the far right. As for the job boredom of some of these men, many of whom will remain vigorous for another 20 years, it seemed to me to suggest the urgency of serious and immediate planning for second career programs in both the public and private sectors, opportunities now limited to more privileged groups where second careers are increasingly pursued.

The older men in our study, those confronting imminent retirement, were not as anxious about their own security or the economic system as middle-aged men, although it should be noted that the field work was conducted prior to the recent sharp inflationary trend and the economic consequences of the "energy crisis." In the early 1970s, these older men felt they had accomplished whatever they could in the way of a financial base for the retirement stage, and they were relatively relaxed about their prospects. Their concerns focused on the development of satisfying post-retirement lifestyles for themselves and their wives, and on ways of making the time left to them as comfortable and easygoing as possible.

However, not all of the men in the middle-aged and preretirement stages were either anomic or hedonistic in their conscious stance toward the future. Roughly, a third of them were in the category which we called "challenged" in a stress typology reported elsewhere (Lowenthal &

Chiriboga, 1973). These men had had and continued to have considerable presumptive stress but did not dwell on it. In many ways they resembled the Type A reported by Friedman and Rosenman (1974) as populations at risk of heart attack or stroke. They are intelligent and the least likely to have developed self-protective lifestyles. Several of these challenged men, however, although judged "well-adapted," were already suffering from rather severe physical impairments. Nevertheless, their own appraisals of their health status were far more optimistic than were those of men who were exposed to much stress and complained at length about it. The challenged men, in fact, seemed to be denying, to themselves and others, that they had any problems at all. One may conclude that their stress reactions are in the physical sphere, whereas those more likely to dwell on their stresses may be of a verbal response type. We conjectured that the complainers (i.e., nonrepressors, or verbal response types) might show a lower morbidity and mortality rate in the future; preliminary analysis of five-year follow-up data does not unequivocally support this prediction.

Stress Perceptions and Stance of Women

On nearly all counts, middle-aged women confronting the postparental period appeared to be in a more critical period than their male counterparts (although women at all stages reported more stressful experiences than men). They were rather inarticulate and diffuse in regard to the stresses accounting for their combination of malaise and anxiety. Although many said they were in general pleased with the prospect of the youngest child leaving home (the next major change they envisaged), they were the most likely of any group to rate the past five years higher than the present and to adopt a more negative stance toward the future. In fact, both women facing the empty nest and those facing the retirement period were altogether more negative and apprehensive about their pending transitions than their male counterparts. However, middle-aged women were more positive about the *past* five years and more negative about the *next* five years than the older women who confronted their husband's retirement and, for about half of these older women, their own retirement as well. The middle-aged women were also far more likely to report an increase in marital problems, a state of affairs not reflected in the reports of their male counterparts nor in those of the older, preretirement women.

Regardless of the amount of presumptive stress to which they had been or continued to be exposed, middle-aged women (average age 48), were the most preoccupied with it, whereas highly stressed middle-aged men were the least so. Middle-aged women had far more psychiatric symptoms than any other subgroup across the four life stages and were most likely to rank low on our adaptive measures. Their low adaptive level was further aggravated if they had experienced parental deprivation in their own early childhoods (this is in contrast to the middle-aged and older men for whom the effects of such deprivation had apparently worn off).

Older women, those confronting retirement (average age 58), were less likely to be suffering from a wide array of symptoms and somewhat less likely to continue to be influenced by parental deprivations than women confronting the empty nest, although they had not caught up with their male age peers in this regard. A significant proportion of these older women were more assertive—for example, more likely to rate themselves fairly high on masculine traits, to call themselves boss in the family, and to be strongly motivated to do something on their own, outside of the family sphere, than those facing the empty nest. At the same time, the older women reported a strange mixture of positive and assertive and negative and passive self-descriptions, as though they were having role conflicts. They were vague and diffuse about what they might actually do. Whereas their motivations seemed stronger than those of the women facing the empty nest, realistic planning was rare, blocked perhaps as much by what they perceived as their husbands' growing dependency needs and demands as by strictures in the world beyond the family. (The five-year follow-up data reinforce the suggestion that the onset of the postparental phase is a critical period for heretofore family-centered women, and that some have resolved the conflict by nurturing their husbands, sometimes bitterly, and others by developing enterprises of their own.)

Resources, Impediments, and Trajectories

Among men there was an increasing tendency across the adult life course for interpersonal factors—the capacity for mutuality in dyadic relationships, many friends, and a broad scope of social roles—to serve as buffers against excessive preoccupation with the past or with stress and to be associated with a relatively positive stance toward the next transition and the future in general.

The trends among women were less clear. For about half of them, the traditional resources of familial roles, familial affect, and a highly feminine self-concept continued to be important. For another group, especially the better educated and more intelligent, such intrapersonal factors as actual competence, a sense of competence, and a positive and more masculine self-image emerged into significance, albeit with some sense of conflict and a feeling of frustration about realistic avenues for self-expression. There was some indication, which finds tentative support in psychoanalytic theory, that these women may have been working through a resurgence of oedipal problems and that those who more or less succeeded in doing so became free to shift roles. Were educational and occupational channels more open, they might well have made and might still make an active contribution to society. Their frustrations tended to resemble those of the challenged men, and presumably their potential life-course trajectories might be similar were they not confronted with so many sociostructural hindrances. These observations reinforce those derived from a detailed analysis of our adaptive indicators: It is the psychologically less complex, who have sought and developed self-protective, stress-avoidant lifestyles, who are aging most happily within our present society.

Trajectories of the more complex women moved in an opposite direction from those of the less complex and more stress-avoidant men. The latter seemed content with what they had accomplished so far and now wanted to relax into a lifestyle of ease and contentment spiked with a bit of hedonism. To the extent that the newly ambitious older women were married to men of this type, it seemed likely that their role conflicts would be resolved, or more likely suppressed, as the need for nurturance on the part of their husbands supplanted that of now departed children. Lacking other outlets, these women were likely to have husbands who complained about their wives' increasing "bossiness" and children who complained about "mom-ism" interference.

Implications for the 21st Century

The policy and planning implications of the results of our studies are that there is a need for life-course orientation in all of our social, educational, and economic institutions. Such educational exposure should begin at least as early as adolescence. In spite of the Women's Liberation Movement and prevalent observations about secular changes in sex roles and in attitudes toward aging, we see as yet few signs of change among the adolescents and young adults in the socioeconomic groups we have been studying. The present and projected lifestyles of these young people continue to remain predominantly family centered and male dominated. As though reflecting on their parents' prospects, they envisage for themselves at postparental and retirement stages little more than financial security, comfort, and freedom from the occupational and familial responsibilities they plan (or believe that they have) to assume and complete in the meantime.

In contrast, one does detect a change among a substantial proportion of students, especially those at the graduate level in academic and professional settings whom many of us observe at first hand. Although they do not comprise a significant segment of the sample being reported on here, it is they who seem to be making innovative changes in regard to traditional sex roles and who are beginning to seek, if not demand, a life-course perspective in the social sciences and in clinical training programs. There is also some encouraging evidence that these value changes, together with cohort shifts in the population, are beginning to be attended by the educational establishment itself. One or two medical schools (and a few psychiatric residency training programs) now require lifespan-oriented courses for their students, for example. Moreover, Dr. Albert Bandura (1974) former president of the American Psychological Association, has recently noted: "As the composition of our population undergoes further changes, lifelong learning is likely to take precedence over degree-seeking in a prescribed period of study."

Such shifts bode well, not for a gerontocracy in the 21st century, but for a society in which those beyond the so-called prime of life (which we suspect may be arriving ever later in the life course) are integrated within its vital institutions rather than sequestered in residential and institutional living quarters limited to their age peers. Until this developmental, if not evolutionary, change takes place in our social structure and institutions, we must hasten to provide some temporary stopgaps, such as serious educational programs for the middle-aged and older people, including those from ethnic minorities and from socioeconomically deprived sectors of our society, which, as we should often remind ourselves, include many gifted and still-growing people whom the Great Depression deprived of an otherwise expectable higher education. Ludicrous though it may sound to many in an achievement-oriented society, large numbers of this generation value learning for its own sake. Were the fields of industry, education, and the mass media not so exclusively youth-oriented, they might well reap enormous benefits with small investments.

Without significant changes of this order we will find ourselves in the 21st century with an increasing proportion of frustrated late middle-aged and young-old people whose personal solution may be to adopt the sick role, thus wreaking a legitimate revenge on the society which has denied them alternatives.

References

Allport, G. W. *Becoming: Basic Considerations for a Psychology of Personality*. New Haven: Yale University Press, 1955.

Bandura, A. Editorial. *APA Monitor*, Feb. 1974, 5(2), 2.

Bühler, C. In C. Bühler & F. Massarik (Eds.), *The Course of Human Life: A Study of Goals in the Humanistic Perspective*. New York: Springer, 1968.

Erikson, E. H. *Dimensions of a New Identity: The Jefferson Lectures in the Humanities*.New York: W. W. Norton, 1974.

Erikson, E. H. *Life History and the Historical Moment*. New York: W. W. Norton, 1975.

Friedman, M. & Rosenman, R. H. *Type A Behavior and Your Heart*. Greenwich, Conn.: Fawcett Publications, 1974.

Fromm, E. *To Have or To Be*. New York: Harper & Row, 1976.

Lowenthal, M. F. & Chiriboga, D. "Social stress and adaptation toward a life course perspective." In Carl Eisdorfer and M. Powell Lawton (Eds.), *The Psychology of Adult Development and Aging*. Washington, D. C.: American Psycholological Association, 1973, pp. 281–310.

Lowenthal, M. F., Thurnher, M., Chiriboga, D., & Associates. *Four Stages of Life: A Comparative Study of Women and Men Facing Transitions*. San Francisco: Jossey-Bass, 1975.

Maslow, A. H. *Motivation and Personality*. New York: Harper & Row, 1954.

Footnotes

[1]Research supported by grants #HD 03051 and HD 05941 from the National Institute of Child Health and Human Development, and currently #AG 00002 from the National Institute on Aging.

Omnia mutantur, et nos mutamur in illis
(All things change and we change with them)

Matthias Borbonius: Deliciae Poetarum Germanorum, I, 685

8

GROUP COMMUNICATION AND GROUP THERAPY WITH THE AGED:
A Promising Project

MARTIN GROTJAHN

America has traditionally been the land of the healthy, the beautiful, and the young. Old people have to compete with young people in being young or appearing to be so, even if it kills them. "Old" used to mean "from the old country." Born Americans of the first generation lived as if they wanted to say: "History begins with us, here in the USA." This led to a denial of old age similar to the denial of death in the American culture. However, this attitude seems to be changing lately. The ever increasing number of senior citizens and the decrease in immigration has led to a reorientation of the general attitude toward the aged and acceptance of needs rarely voiced before.

The literature contains relatively few guidelines for psychiatry or psychotherapy in the field of gerontology. Butler (1975; see also Butler & Lewis, 1976) points out that old people can get as hysterical as young people, only it shows differently. According to him, 80% of all analytic patients are 45 years of age or younger. Old people do not come to psychiatrists.

Butler's claim that psychoanalysis rarely accepts old people for treatment may be true and one is tempted to answer to that: "What do old people need a new transference neurosis for?" In other words, individual treatment may not be the answer for the psychiatric problems of the aged. Even where psychoanalysis or individual treatment is feasible for financial reasons, it may not necessarily be the treatment of choice. The implied negative answer to that question, in turn, suggests the need for a positive approach to problems that continue to persist.

Group Therapy for the Aged

I envision teams of experts with and without medical background and training, who would go to the homes of old people and conduct group sessions there. Perhaps the term "group therapy" may sound too ambitious or even misleading, for old age in itself is not a psychiatric illness. The function of these teams of therapists could be seen in establishing group communication and they could be designated as "communicators."

Optimally, group therapy leads immediately to relief of depression, loneliness, and the feeling of being rejected by the family. The sharing of common worries would help to form group cohesion. Old age therefore could be a satisfactory stage of the life cycle. The time may come when old people will say: "The last years of my life were the best."

Group communication and therapy could realize such a utopian hope.

In such groups, the transference situation, which is the foundation of all treatment, is quite different from that in any individual relationship. In the group, members form a new transference relationship to the therapist (or the team of therapists), to their peers, and to the group as such, which may include the institutions in which the old people live. Such a "divided" transference cannot reach the intensity of a transference neurosis as is essential to standard psychoanalysis (Grotjahn, 1977).

Lissy Jarvik (1975), in her pioneering studies of old age, shows that continued mental activity is necessary to avoid the main conflicts of aging. Inactivity, both physical and mental, results in deterioration. Group therapy offers continued mental activity. In the individual psychotherapy the patient may continue his or her loneliness, develop further dependency, remain inactive, and feel guilty about it. Group therapy gives almost immediate relief to these symptoms that accompany aging.

If the group therapist has started group communication he or she has fulfilled his or her first assignment. A second assignment would be to induce the group not to deny aging and to accept life as it has been lived. Hand in hand with that goes the final acceptance of death as a natural end of human existence.

There is no reason to glorify old age, nor is there any reason to deny it. One has to accept the past before one can accept the present. This acceptance should be prepared for throughout all of life. People should be aware that they have to live with their pasts. If they could be aware of this they would probably have a better chance of avoiding old-age depressions. Americans like to live quite generally in the "existential moment." They do not live for the future as they do not like to live in the past; both avoidances make adjustment to old age difficult.

One great difficulty for the therapist arises here: How shall a therapist accept people who should not and cannot be accepted because they have lived lives of selfishness? It sometimes helps to show them that all human mistakes, short of murder, can be undone.

When a depressed person is rooted in a group, the initial stage of therapy has been mastered: that person is no longer all alone. Then suicide rarely, if ever, happens. Any one who has ever worked with groups will agree that group therapy is the treatment of choice for depression, including suicidal depression, at any age.

There are essential differences in the tasks of mastering infancy, childhood, adolescence, maturity, and old age, which is the sublimation of maturity to wisdom. Whereas maturity implies mastery of inner and outer reality, wisdom implies mastery of the existential limitation of human life. Wisdom is the willing acceptance of death as an existential fact.

Some Facts of Life

Besides his or her skill as a group communicator, the group therapist would do well to keep a few psychological facts in mind when treating the aged. As children have to learn the facts of life, so old people must learn some facts of long life. One old woman once told me with bitterness, but also with some humor: "Nobody ever told me that I, too, would grow old."

Old people have to learn about changes in their sexuality and the group therapist must know about them. One of the first misunderstandings that has to be corrected is that which arises from reading Masters and Johnson (1966). There is not much gained by asking old men about their sexual potency. They almost always lie, the way they used to do in puberty. The standard answer is: "If you want to know whether I am too old to be potent, then you must ask somebody older." It is somewhat more promising to ask the partners of old people.

In the first place, a man reaching an age between 60 and 65 needs an "inviting female." What used to be a joy in former times now becomes a necessity.

Second, men have to accept retardation in all sexual functions. They have to learn that it is possible and necessary to enjoy sex without ejaculation but still with orgasm.

Third, sexual pleasure frequently changes in character and turns to a kind of spectator sport. It is astonishing to see that gray- and white-haired people of both sexes enjoy pornographic movies or strip teases; they often constitute the majority of the audience.

The group therapist must know how to correct two misunderstandings: old people do not live beyond "sin" and they must not expect to function unchanged. Here, the sexual superiority of women becomes obvious once more.

A tragic difference in the sexual behavior of men and women must be mentioned here. Old men are frequently attractive to young women and, as a rule, with some skill, have no difficulties in finding sexual or semisexual partners; younger women are attracted by older men who represent the father to them. This incest taboo is never absolute. Older women are rarely attractive to younger men because the old woman is the symbol of the mother, and as such she is sexually taboo. This is a strict and almost absolutely enforced taboo. However, these are not innate psychological conditions. Older women can be attractive and often are, but the taboo forbids younger men to look at older women as sexual objects. It is possible that in the future, when our multiorgiastic young female generation will have grown old, a new attitude of sexual equality of the aged can be established.

One last point must be made: Group therapy offers the possibility of discussing problems of death and dying in a much less emotional way than in individual dialog. Discussions of death between two people soon lead to embarrassment, guilt, and silence. This is not the case in group discussions.

However, talking about death should not be forced. The therapist must allow it to happen and must be prepared. A good place to learn how to deal with such discussion is in groups of terminally ill people. When they have felt initial relief and have gone through the stage of complaining about their environments, about the nurses who are unfriendly and overworked, about the physicians who always rush away, about the medicine that is never strong enough, about the sedation that is always given too late, about the family they feel has deserted them (which gives the first meetings the character of unpleasant, boring bull sessions), then a more fruitful and constructive stage of group therapy will be reached and deeper anxieties can be debated. The problem of death will then move into focus.

The first signs of concern with death may become visible in dreams. The therapist should be familiar with the symbols of death. It is tragic that people's most beautiful dreams are usually dreams of death. Beauty and color are the most frequent symbols of death in dreams, but there are many.

An old man once told his group the following dream, which started with great beauty and ended in a frightful nightmare: The old man dreamed that he took a walk with his grandson, three or four years old. They walked together and came to a high cliff with a balustrade protecting them from falling into a deep and wide canyon below. Both the old man and his little grandson stood still and looked down and saw below them a green valley of indescribable beauty. There was a little pond which was obviously left over from the drying out of a larger lake. It was surrounded by lush green vegetation. On the water, lotus and water lilies were blooming. A most beautiful bird was standing at one end of the pond. He had all kinds of gleaming colors and was built somewhat like a blue heron. There was a second bird standing at the opposite end of the lake. The little boy wanted to see better, so he swung himself on top of the balustrade, lost hold, flew over it, and fell down, probably to his death. The old man was horrified, hollered for help, and woke up.

The old man was disturbed because he was sophisticated enough to suspect death wishes against the child in himself, which he could not accept. The association showed that the boy symbolized the dreamer's own youth, which had to die. He had to accept the fact that he is old now and getting older. He then realized that the bird was the mythical phoenix which dies and is reborn from the ashes. That was the reason why there was a second bird, the reincarnation of the first one. The pond is the place all life comes from.

A word of caution may be indicated about any statements concerning "the right to die" in groups of the aged. I have learned not to make any remarks in favor of euthanasia. My attitude will always be on the side of life. I try to analyze the wish to die as a hostility turned against one's self, or as an accusation against the family. As long as somebody asks for help to die he or she is not ready for it.

Immediately after group sessions medical attention should be available to the group members. Every group session may as well end with medical response to the complaints of its members. This may concern the usual complaints about constipation, sleeplessness, weight loss or gain, lack of appetite, or hypertension. If these questions are treated after the group session, it gives additional stimulus to continued participation. All medical problems should be heard but then referred from the session to the time after the group.

Therapists who work with the elderly must analyze and understand their own attitudes toward old people and their own parents, in particular. Such therapists should not be unduly loving, nor have a need to idealize members of the group, nor dislike them.

Therapists must be able to stand the great love of their old patients, and must be able to accept this love as an expression of their attitude: "My time is mostly over, I will live in you, my therapist, and therefore I love you." Therapists must be able to withstand great hostility, which grows out of the bitter resentment: "I have to go and you will live." Therapists will also find it easier to deal with their responses to these emotions in group rather than in individual sessions.

Group therapy is a great hope for the aged. It also could be a great promise for the final maturation of the therapist who wants to accomplish with the patient the ultimate lesson that the therapist, too, must learn—namely, growing old gracefully.

References

Butler, R. *Why Survive ? Being Old in America.* New York: Harper & Row, 1975.

Butler, R. & Lewis, M. *Sex After Sixty: A Guide for Men and Women for Their Later Years.* New York: Harper & Row, 1976.

Grotjahn, M. *The Art and Technique of Analytic Group Therapy.* New York: Jason Aronson, 1977.

Jarvik, L. Thoughts on the psychobiology of aging. *American Psychologist.* 1975, *30*(5): 576–583.

Masters, W. H. & Johnson, V. *The Human Sexual Response.* Boston: Little, Brown, 1966.

Good, the more communicated,
more abundant grows

John Milton, Paradise Lost, Book V. line 71

9

SOCIETAL RESPONSE TO AGING:
Some Possible Consequences

CARL EISDORFER

In this chapter I plan to discuss possible consequences of societal response to aging, including problems and opportunities engendered by the projected change in the composition of our society in the next few decades, as well as training strategies to meet these challenges. To accomplish those ends I will orient you to my methodology and discuss alternative situations for which we might need to prepare ourselves.

In approaching this presentation, three strategies seemed most appropriate. The first, and most parsimonious, attempts to develop from current population trends a projection into the 21st century, while remaining fairly conservative in the anticipation of any changes in basic human psychology, biological needs, capacities, and lifestyles. Change would be programmed only on the basis of patterns currently observable. Such an approach, through statistical projection, has considerable appeal in the interest of accuracy, if only a minimal amount of excitement. It is necessarily limited by the nature and validity of the data base relevant to the areas in which the prediction is to be made. For population trends it seems a reasonable enough approach. For economic data it is of somewhat more tenuous validity, and for predicting patterns of behavior it is based on having handles on an exquisitely small proportion of the total variance.

Probably the most accurate statement which could be made is that there will be little, if any, change in our culture, including the social role of the aged, within the next several decades. This assumes no significant change in adult life expectancy or in exit age from the labor force and no major economic upheavals. Because there will be more aged persons we will need more service personnel, it is hoped with better training, and we look forward to an improvement in our capacity to deal with the range of unmet needs currently exhibited by the aged. Increased numbers of better trained individuals could help us modify the "all-or-none" strategy of service delivery and we would see improved patterns of community-and home-based care.

An alternative strategy would focus on the subjective or impressionistic data base of a few gifted individuals extraordinarily sensitive to interpersonal interactions and imaginative enough to make logical or at least plausible statements about the future. If this sounds like pseudoscience, or even fiction and science fiction at that, then you may be accused of predicting my behavior, in this instance, with some accuracy.

A third major approach to the problem of evaluating

alternatives is to use consensual validation. This distinguished research approach is used by many of us in the social and behavioral sciences when, in the absence of an empirical understanding of reality, we can at least develop a friendly agreement as to the nature of unreality. Instead of attempting to rigidify this creative approach by using questionnaires and statistical tests of significance, I felt that the more popular form of consensual validation might suffice. For the last several months, therefore, at every reasonable opportunity during the course of casual conversations, I have secretly polled educated specialists in a variety of scientific fields, as well as an ample supply of sensitive and articulate human beings whose current activities are too complicated to allow an abbreviated description.

Not satisfied with these three significant approaches to the problem, I attempted to engage myself in reviewing some of the literature of the futurologists and planners, becoming quite impressed with the astute observations and insights that many of them make concerning the nature of the future and how we can effectively orient ourselves to it, or avoid it.

By way of a loose framework of constraints, I would like to remind us that any individual or group of individuals can be evaluated in terms which focus primarily on their contributions to a society, as well as on their utilization of its resources. These dimensions, giving and taking as it were, are not simple and discrete, however, but often rather elusive and occasionally overlapping. Thus, the emotional contributions of children to adults are hard to assess in measurable units; and consumerism or consumption patterns, even as practiced by the aged, may play an essential and therefore contributory role in an economy. What seems clear is that the balance of input and outgo shifts in relation to age. The young receive more resources than they generate, perhaps as a means of investing in the continued future of the social unit. The working group generates products and services, not only for itself but for other segments of the population. The postwork group receives in some rough approximation to their past social status instead of in terms of current contribution. It is clear that the role of the aged can be associated with the issues of the balance of contribution in relationship to utilization of societal resources.

It should be recognized, however, that "old," or "aged," in our society is defined in a remarkably arbitrary way. Biologically, little distinguishes individuals during the postadolescence age span. In our country, the 65th birthday has become the entry point into older age, largely on the basis of a social security system that set up this age initially in an effort to alter the size of the labor force and unemployment statistics during depression years. As mentioned several times, this group of the population will continue to increase in number and proportion for at least the next few decades.

Over the past half-century, lifespan at birth has increased impressively and it is still growing, albeit by increasingly smaller amounts. Although adult lifespan has been altered far less radically, with major inroads in the management of significant diseases of adult life and most particularly of cardiovascular disease, I think we can fully anticipate that lifespan beyond age 65 will be greatly lengthened in the foreseeable future, thus yielding a significant increase in the number and proportion of older persons beyond what is currently anticipated. Far more important is the fact that the increase likely to occur will be in the older segment of the old age group.

As is often pointed out, the "aged" is too broad an age category. Often the "aged" are coalesced as if they represented a homogeneous group, which indeed they do not. All of our data indicate that for most variables the variance increases with increasing age past early maturity; and thus the aged are less alike than are people at any other time in their lifespan. The result is that it is very difficult to make blanket statements about the aged, per se, or the needs of the aged except in the most general terms. We should, ideally, focus on special subgroups of the aged and their needs, but recognize that some of the problems of the aged may be generated by society's conglomerate definition and the strategies it has developed as a result of that biased definition.

Let us focus on a few specific issues: health, work, economics, social status, education, value of life, value of living, and the cadre of people being specifically trained to serve the aged of the future. As has been described, the number and proportion of over 65-year-olds in our society will grow to about 29 million, or more than 12% of the population of the United States by the end of the century. The absolute number will continue to escalate beyond that, although the percentage may plateau, assuming, however, that the definition of older age is stable at age 65. This assumption is, of course, not necessarily valid, for older age is a mixed biological, psychological, and social event. Retirement at age 60 or age 55 could substantially alter the situation. Given current economic projections and increased unemployment, the likelihood of an even more substantial increase in the proportion of the population that is retired seems reasonable. Such persons may be technically unemployable but may be physically in reasonably good health and may constitute a cadre of individuals whose energy allows participation in a variety of activities, including a new wave of political awareness that may emerge. Future cohorts of the aged will undoubtedly include more and more healthy, educated, and politically active members of our society and, with their attention not focused on somatic state, a shift from the relative political passivity of today's elderly may well occur. I think that in the absence of heightened consumer potential this is a most reasonable possibility.

Obviously, societal needs could modify this proposition. With a sudden shift in population growth, we could find ourselves in need of an enlarged labor force in a few years and a desire to reemploy the aged might arise. A social pattern of part time employment of many older persons and a heightened requirement for older adult educators could well parallel such a general upsweep in the economy.

Perhaps the most significant issue to which we should attend is the possibility of a major alteration in the lifespan for older adults. Attaining prevention for cancer would add only approximately three years to lifespan at birth with half that time added to the life expectancy of the 65-year-old. Elimination of death caused by cardiovascular illness would result in a substantial increase in life expectancy, that is, 10.8 years, at birth. Impressively, 10.4 of those years would be added to life expectancy at 65. Using current figures, approximately 1.54 million Americans reach the age of 65 each year with one million deaths due to all causes. The result is a net increase of about 540,000 persons per year. An increase of ten years in life expectancy at age 65 would result in a cadre of approximately 5.5 million older old persons surviving into advanced age over and above currently anticipated growth. Reaching 65, they would then have a life expectancy of approximately 90 years.

It is important to appreciate at this point that the health problems, and particularly the mental health problems, of older persons are directly related to age past 65. Thus, three-fourths of all older persons have a chronic illness, 47% have some limitation in activities of daily life, and 38% have some significant impairment in their ability to function. Chronic brain syndrome or senile dementia alone, which has a prevalence rate of approximately 3% during the age span of 60 through 69, increases by more than sixfold to age 90, where it reaches a prevalence rate of approximately 20%. Estimates for mental and emotional disorders among the aged run from a low of 15% to a high of approximately 30% in the 65+ age group, and although the data are relatively sparse, the conjecture is that risk increases with age. Nursing home bed utilization doubles with every decade of life past the 60s. With a 20% to 25% increase in the aged population added to the later years of life, therefore, the result should be an approximate doubling of bed use for long-term care, as well as use of more than half of our general hospital bed days by persons over 65.

A caveat is in order, however, since the difficulties in making these projections are secondary to the ambiguity of the current method of evaluating data concerning the aged population. Very often we are presented with the age category "65" without further breakdown so that predicting to the state or needs of age groups 70 to 80, or from 80 to 90 or beyond is still in the realm of sophisticated crystal gazing and extrapolated from more or less relevant findings.

To add to this complexity, we do not have data, for example, on the salutary effects of modifying cardiovascular diseases, the influence on general health and well-being, cognitive functioning, or other diseases that may reduce the need for services. Additionally, some of these diseases of older persons may be treatable. However, research in this area is conspicuously absent.

Statistics aside, an insidiously emerging issue is whether any society will continue to bear the economic and social consequences posed by an increasing group of dependent, nonproductive, and never to be productive individuals. Given the current dysutility of older persons in our society, the problem will be compounded by the rapid rate at which they will utilize recognizably finite resources of a developing and controlling majority, while adding no economic benefits of their own.

Because we are constantly amazed at the validity of the H. G. Wellses of the past, I feel it would be valuable to turn to a popular science fiction novelist of the present, Kurt Vonnegut, whose insights and fantasies concerning the social status of the elderly could well be evaluated in a future projection. In his "Welcome to the Monkey House," Vonnegut's (1974) solution to the dilemma of humanitarianism versus competition for resources lies in the ethical suicide society. Will the future develop social pressures on individuals, confronting them with the need to avail themselves of a "humane" alternative to overpopulating the planet? This behavior would be no more demanding than the pre-Social Security Eskimo cultures, in which the aged hunter would continue his search for game, not returning without a kill, whereas the younger man could return empty handed with the knowledge that he was fit to go out another time and that he would probably continue to make a positive contribution to the group.

Such a choice is not that remote. Prolongation of life, once an inviolate if unexpressed code of the health professions, is now under reconsideration in the light of the recognized and often clerically sanctioned need of persons to die with dignity. Living wills instructing physicians not to use extraordinary means to prolong life are available for the interested and many are interested.

What do we train for in this instance? Vonnegut recognizes the need for a highly trained elitist cadre of attractive young women and men to serve the parlors of the ethical suicide society. Doubtless, these guides will need basic information in pharmacology or electronics, along with nursing, interview, and psychological training to help calm the anxiety of those who have changes of heart. Perhaps a portion of the curriculum of airline steward(ess) charm schools might also be of value here.

A more immediately pragmatic alternative in our society would be to redevelop the elderly as a group which would contribute to the greater good, possibly as a consumer group. If Kreps' (1971) ideas concerning redistribution of lifespan earnings would take effect, the elderly might become very valuable consumers. Given increased resources, the dollar amounts they would expend could be impressive. At the moment, the aged are already a target for a limited number of entrepreneurs, including travel agents, vitamin and laxative purveyors, and those in the rejuvenating business. As long as they have adequate resources, societal pressures to keep them alive and to keep them spending money may remain high in the interests of the overall economy. It remains necessary to provide these resources and find a relatively noninflationary way to support a nonproductive group with a stable proportion of the Gross National Product (GNP), instead of a fixed income with reduced spending value in the face of a rising GNP and increasing inflation.

Another possibility is to reexamine the current pattern of distribution of work and the investment of educational resources through the lifespan. There may be a need to reevaluate the concept of one person per job, or of a single trajectory career ladder with the dominant portion of education and training at the point before entry.

Often without adequate educational resources, the elderly move into unplanned obsolescence in a pattern whereby the young are given access to emerging data for survival while the elderly are left to search for it on their own. This is both a symptomatic and etiologic issue.

Perhaps midcareer shifts should be programmed with retirement for a given occupation anticipated every decade and followed by a retraining period. The implication of this strategy for the educational enterprise would be profound, and strategies of adult and continuing education would need reconceptualization in the face of extraordinarily high numbers of involved adults who might wish to participate in the educational system on a different basis from the current secondary school or undergraduate student.

The notion of a sabbatical for all workers with the sabbatical being programmed as an educational experience needs serious consideration. In this framework, retirement at a younger age might be subordinated to the concept of recertification or reorientation to enhance one's life and work. Such professions as medicine are already feeling pressured in this direction and ongoing professional education and recertification as a part of professional life is on the horizon for most physicians. The concept of a career lattice as a replacement for the career ladder would be an interesting consequence, and lateral or parallel rather than a narrow upward mobility may be among the ways of the future.

A strategy of redefining retirement and an educational process that does not terminate with adolescence but allows and stimulates adults to initiate new lifestyles should have profound social and psychological consequences. Maintenance of an age-integrated social system and the prevention of cognitive decline are only a few of the possible consequences of such a pattern and the sharing of roles by old, middle-aged, and young individuals should do much to dispel the illusion of a generation gap. The need for vocational counselors and an array of tests and measurements would increase, and aptitude-and-interest-testing battery makers would have a field day in such a culture. Clearly, difficulties lie in the possible abuses of such a socially engineered society where care must be taken that choice not be subordinated to placement by fiat. It would be essential to maximize freedom of choice, and the alternative options would always need to be available.

In closing, let me comment that we are currently seeing several active waves of change. In a society where the social stigmata of old age were to be removed, the elderly might well be the most outspoken and vigorous leaders of social change. This might do a great deal to eradicate the impression that older persons are politically rigid and conservative and would even get rid of the fantasy that we need to worry about a gerontocracy. Large groups of the aged today are becoming healthier, more affluent, and more articulate as the cohorts of the aged will have had greater advantages during their youth. At the same time, we are seeing very little being done to plan for the long-term health care needs associated with advancing age. We see few provisions for the training of individuals suited for coping with the unique physical and emotional difficulties so prevalent among the aged as a result of multiple illness and social assaults; and little effort is being made toward preventing disease and toward research in the processes of aging.

Nevertheless, my chronic optimism leads me to feel that there are very exciting solutions to the social dilemma of an earmarked dependent group of the population, a major portion of whose skills are now largely wasted. The possibility of continued social dysutility; the high rates of depression and physical disorder; the high risk for mental, emotional, and cognitive loss; the chronic lack of resources and inability to keep up with a growing inflationary economy could, in the absence of significant change in social role, require new strategies. Such strategies would probably not be imposed on the aged by the younger society but might be taken upon themselves by a segment of the aged population. Let me remind you that the risk of suicide among white elderly males is sixteenfold higher than it is among younger persons. Significant lengthening of life in the absence of appropriate alterations in social roles, health supports, income, education, and the ability to make a contribution to the broader society may well lead to the widespread conclusion among the elderly that life itself is not enough. The impact of such a realization on the young as well as on the aged should not be underestimated. To that extent, one may legitimately say that in our treatment of the elderly we have a mirror of our total society.

References

Some demographic aspects of aging in the United States. A U. S. Department of Commerce Publication, Series P-23, No. 43, February 1973.

Kreps, J. M. *Lifetime Allocation of Work and Income: Essays in the Economics of Aging*. Durham, N.C.: Duke University Press, 1971.

Vonnegut, Kurt, Jr., *Welcome to the Monkey House*. New York: Dell, 1974.

Yet who would have thought the old man
to have had so much blood in him?

Macbeth, Act V, Sc 1, line 42

10

THE FUTURE AND THE YOUNG-OLD*

BERNICE L. NEUGARTEN

A wide range of predictions regarding the future of our society and the future of the world have been put before the American public in the past few years. In the flood of statements that are now appearing there are—to oversimplify it—perspectives that are grandly optimistic, others that are grossly pessimistic. The economy will continue to expand, and the good life will soon be here for us all, or the economy is on the verge of collapse. With continued growth of science and technology, man will solve the problems of overpopulation, food shortages, energy crises, inflation, environmental pollution, and the threat of nuclear war; or because of the very growth of science and technology, such problems are now so unprecedented in scale that man's efforts are doomed to fail.

Within one or the other perspective, the future status

*Abridged from *The Gerontologist*, 1975, *15*, 1–9.

of the aged is also differently described. In the optimistic world-view, where at least the developed countries are moving from a production orientation to a quality-of-life orientation, it is said that more equitable social systems are arising. Older persons will get their fair share of the new abundance. In the pessimistic view, where among other things there will be increasing alienation, conflict over employment opportunities and competition between age groups, the old will become newly disadvantaged.

We ourselves have taken a mid-way position, one we regard as conservatively optimistic, and one that might be called a view of the relatively "normal, expectable future." This we regard as the most expeditious view in furthering our own more circumscribed approach to futures research.

In very brief terms, we are assuming that for the American society there will be slowed economic growth together with slowed population growth, with Zero Population Growth occurring in about 50 years; increasing urbanization and growth of metropolitan agglomerations; continuing technological advances and an increasingly rapid rate of their application. Levels of education will continue to rise, although at a less dramatic rate than in the past few decades, producing less difference between age groups.

We are assuming a value orientation which—to borrow a phrase from Denis Johnston (1972) and others—is neither the "blue" world of the work ethic nor the "green" world of the leisure ethic, but a "turquoise" world in which new concepts of work and new flexible life styles will appear, so that in both the work setting and the leisure setting there will be greater concern for personal growth and fulfillment. We are presuming also a society in which there will be more, rather than less planning, and in which the role of government in the affairs of everyday life will increase rather than decrease. We are assuming that persons of all ages will expect "more" from life, although "more" may mean a changing value system in which the pursuit of affluence may become less significant than the pursuit of meaningful ways of self-enhancement and community enhancement.

How Many Older Persons Will There Be?

Whatever the uncertainties in other areas, population projections for the middle-aged and old are relatively safe for the next 25 years because they depend on mortality rates, not fertility rates. Everybody who will be old by the year 2000 is already alive. But will he live a great deal longer than his predecessors?

Two general strategies for lengthening life are being pursued by biomedical and biological researchers: the first is the continuing effort to conquer major diseases; the other, to alter the intrinsic biological processes which are presumed to underlie aging and which may proceed independently from disease processes—that is, to discover the genetic and biochemical secrets of aging, then to slow the biological clock that is presumably programmed into the human species. This second approach is directed at rate control, rather than disease control.

Thus far all the increases in life expectancy have been due to increased controls over disease but not, so far as is known, to any decrease in the rate of aging. The question then becomes, are there likely to be dramatic discoveries with regard to rate control that will lead to a mushrooming in numbers of older persons by the year 2000?

In attempting to answer this question, we have made inquiries of leading biological researchers, asking for their assessments. With the striking exception of a few who are saying that if research efforts were generously enough supported, the life-span could be extended some 20 to 25 years within the next two decades, for example, Comfort (1959) and Strehler (1970), the responses we have thus far received are consistently negative. The overwhelming majority have responded that they see no such possibility. We have therefore proceeded on the conservative view that there will be no dramatic changes in the length of the human life span within the next few decades, but that, instead, there will be relatively regular improvements with regard to medical knowledge and health care that will produce steady but slow reduction in mortality rates. McFarland has calculated the numbers of older persons who will be alive in the year 2000 if age-specific mortality rates were to fall by 2% per year for all persons aged 20+.

This projection may be overly optimistic, for it will depend upon improved health practices such as reduced cigarette smoking and reduced consumption of foods that increase the likelihood of heart disease, as well as upon reduction in atmospheric pollution and improved health services. This projection has seemed to us not unreasonable, however, in light of the most recent data on heart disease in United States, as well as other health data for this and other countries. In any case, McFarland's figures serve to show the cumulative effect of a relatively

conservative improvement in mortality rates if that improvement continues from year to year. For example, the
65+ population in the year 2000 is expected to be about
26.5 million under present mortality rates, but about 35.5
million under the reduced rates. For the 75+ population
the difference is even greater, for the number would be
under 12 million in the one instance, but over 18 million in
the other instance.

Thus, a 2% per year reduction in mortality rates would
add about 5 years to average life expectancy for persons
aged 65. Men who reached 65 in 1970 could expect, on the
average, to live to 78; but men who reach age 65 in 2000
could expect to live to 83 (the parallel figures for women
are 81.5 and 86).

What Will Be the Health Status of Older People?

Given our assumption that average life expectancy will
increase over the next 25 years, and the assumption that
this increase will come, not from a slowing of the rate of
aging, but from continuingly improved health, it follows
that we are also assuming improved health status for older
persons in the future.

In truth, the realities are more complex. The relations
of various forms of morbidity to mortality are not well
understood, nor the relations of mortality rates at younger
ages to mortality rates at later ages; there are various def-
initions of "health" or "vigor" and various indices that
have been used for measurement; levels of education and
socioeconomic status are related both to morbidity and

mortality, and so on. Suffice it to say that for the future we are presuming better levels of health for older persons because poverty is diminishing over the life-cycles of successive cohorts of persons, because educational levels are rising, and because we predict more effective forms of public health and improved systems of health care.

All this says little, however, regarding the period of disability that can be expected to occur for many people in the very last phase of life; and for the moment, we have little basis for predicting that this period will become shorter.

What Will Be the Role of the Family?

Keeping in mind that "family" is not synonymous with "household," and looking first at family structure, it is clear from census data that there has been a significant shift in marital status of older persons in the past 20 years, with an increase in the proportions of both men and women who are married and living with spouse present, and with offsetting decreases in the proportions never married, widowed, or divorced. Whether these trends will continue into the next 25 years will depend upon a whole host of factors, social as well as economic, not least upon changing attitudes toward marriage, divorce, and remarriage. Some observers believe that nontraditional forms of family life and various manifestations of women's liberation are spreading rapidly into the present middle-aged group; and if so, these will carry forward into old age by the decade 1990-2000, but in fact such evidence as is presently available indicates that the "nonmarried" family, the commune, and other such family forms constitute a very tiny proportion even of the present-day young.

With regard to intergenerational family structure, we can be fairly sure that the four- and five-generation family will be the norm because of increasing longevity and because the length of generations has been shortening.

It is often overlooked that for persons who will be old in 2000, there will be more, rather than fewer children and other relatives. According to McFarland's projections, it appears that the woman who will reach 55 in the year 2000 will have more surviving children than the women who reached 55 in 1975; and that for women who will reach 75, the increases will be even more striking. These projections are based on stable mortality rates throughout the next 25 years, but the differences reflect, of course, the fluctuating birth rates of past decades. (If, as was suggested earlier, mortality rates are reduced in the future, the rates of surviving children will be further affected.)

Numbers of surviving children do not, of course, tell us about interactions or patterns of assistance between parent and child. Projections of the latter type are difficult. We do not, for example, have national data for the 1970s similar to those for the 1960s reported by Shanas, Townsend, Wedderburn, Friis, Milhoj, and Stehouwer (1968) by which to assess present patterns of family interaction, to say nothing of future patterns. Yet a whole range of smaller studies leads to the conclusion that the family has thus far remained a strong and supportive institution for older people. Our review of this literature adds up to the following: most old people want to be independent of their families as much as possible, but when they can no longer manage for themselves, they expect their children to come to their aid. Not only do such expectations exist, but they are usually met. A complex pattern of exchange of services exists across generations, and both ties of affection and ties of obligation remain strong. Perhaps expectations will change in these regards by the year 2000, but if so, the changes are likely to be slow.

When it comes to living in the same household, there has been a dramatic trend toward separate households for older persons. While there are more families having older relatives, fewer are living with them. Yet even as late as 1970, the latest year for which national data are available, it was clear that the older the individual, and the sicker, the more likely he would be found living with a child. For all persons aged 75+, one of five women, and one of ten men were living with a child (a few percent were living with another relative). It is a neglected fact that, in 1970, a total of 2¼ million persons aged 65+ were living in the same household with a child or other relative.

Here again it is not easily predicted whether or not the trend toward separate households will continue. The trends will be affected by economic factors and by housing policies. One significant factor is the increasing numbers of families in which persons of advanced old age have children who are themselves old, a trend that will become even more marked in the next few decades. What its effects will be is difficult to foresee. If a more effective network of supportive social and home health services arises, more intergenerational households may appear in which both generations are old.

One thing is likely: that families will want more options

in the settings and types of care available for an aged family member whose health is failing. Such institutions as nursing homes may be necessary for a part of the population, but many families may seek ways of maintaining an older person at home, either in his own household or in the child's household.

The Young-Old

We suggest that the age of retirement—or, perhaps more accurately, the age of "first retirement"—will come about age 55 in the year 2000 rather than, as now, at about age 65. With the anticipated increase in life expectancy the post retirement period of the lifespan for men will be about 25 to 28 years instead of the present 13 years. The implications of this change, together with various other sets of data regarding the characteristics of older persons, suggest a meaningful division between the "young-old" and the "old-old."

Although it is life styles rather than chronological ages that concern us, nevertheless most of the young-old can be expected to come from the group who are 55 to 75, and most of the old-old, from those who are 75+.

Age 55 is beginning to be a meaningful age marker in the life-cycle because of the lowering age of retirement. The large majority of persons now retiring are doing so earlier than "required" by mandatory rules, with many retiring just as soon as they can live comfortably on their retirement incomes. One example is the auto workers who exercise the option to retire at 55. In an increasing number of occupational groups, eligibility for pensions is determined not by age, but by numbers of years of service, with the result that some men are retiring in their early 50s or even earlier. In other industries, where over-all employment is declining, the downward trend in age of retirement is dramatic. The 1970 census already shows only 81% of all 55- to 64-year-old men in the labor force, compared to 92% in the next younger age group.

The trend toward earlier retirement will depend upon rates of economic and technological growth, international as well as national, the numbers of young workers, the number of women workers, the extent to which the work setting becomes more attractive, the adequacy of retirement income, the value of leisure time, and so on. But most observers predict that the downward trend in age of retirement will continue over the next two or three decades. By and large, the young-old will become increasingly a group of retirees.

As suggested by our earlier comments on health status, the young-old are already a relatively healthy group. The data have not been aggregated in age categories most appropriate to our purposes, but at present, about 15% of the group aged 45 to 64 need to limit their major activities because of health, while for all those 65+, it is about 40%. We estimate that, if our young-old group were differentiated in these data, the proportion with health limitations would probably be between 20 and 25%.

In distinguishing further between the young-old and the old-old, and in looking at the population data and the family data we see that women outnumber men by a sizable proportion, but less so in the 55+ and 65+ than in the 75+. Furthermore, because most men marry women somewhat younger than themselves, the young-old as a total group are more like younger than like older age-groups. About 80% of the young-old men, and well over half the women were married in 1970 and living with their spouses. By far the common pattern is the husband and wife living in their own household, with some 80% owning their own homes.

The economic status of the young-old is less easily assessed. For most persons income drops precipitously upon retirement, and if present trends continue, the adjustment to lower incomes may be timed closer to age 55 than to age 65. The anticipation of a longer period of life at a reduced income may affect monetary savings plans in young adulthood just as it affects pension plans, but such consequences are presently unpredictable. However, current income is only part of total economic resources. (For instance, government in-kind transfers such as Medicare, value of rent to homeowners, net worth holdings, tax adjustments, intrafamily transfers, and other components need to be included in assessing economic well-being.) It is an open question whether, in the next few decades, economic well-being will be increasingly equalized across age groups, but the trend has clearly been thus far toward improved economic status for older people.

It is likely that economic hazards for both the young-old and the old-old will be further reduced in the near future. Threats of inflation notwithstanding, the rises in Social Security together with their cost-of-living increases, and the new federalization of the welfare system (the Supplemental Security Income System that makes the incomes of the poorest older people somewhat more adequate than before) together constitute one major step forward. It is almost certain also that a form of national health insurance will soon be instituted which will meet an increasing proportion of health costs for persons of all ages. In addition, private and public pensions and profit-sharing plans have spread, and greater numbers of workers will collect benefits, given the newest federal legislation that monitors the operation of private pension plans. To the extent these and other changes occur, the major threats to economic well-being of older persons will be effectively diminished, with the outcome that the future young-old should be more financially secure than their predecessors.

The young-old are already much better educated than the old-old, and in the near future they will be in a less disadvantaged position in comparison to the young. The gains in educational level in successive cohorts of the population have been so substantial that by 1990 the young-old group will be, on the average, high school graduates. Furthermore, with the anticipated growth in higher education for adults, whether degree-oriented or not, and the even greater growth in what the Carnegie Commission (1973) calls "further education" (that education, both part-time and full-time, which occurs in settings other than college campuses and which is not aimed at academic degrees) it can be anticipated that the educational differences that presently exist between young, middle-aged, and young-old will be further reduced.

With regard to political participation, the young-old group is a highly active group compared to other age groups. Verba and Nie (1972) show that, when their national data are corrected for income and education, overall political participation is highest for the age group 51-65 (i.e., voting, persuading others how to vote, actively working for party or candidate, working with others on local problems); and it falls off only a little for persons over 65. Thus, in the electorate as a whole the young-old are disproportionately influential.

What Will the Young-Old Want?

These, then, are some of the characteristics of that 15% of the total population who are the young-old. As a group, they are already markedly different from the out-moded stereotypes of old age. They are relatively free from traditional social responsibilities of work and family, they are relatively healthy, relatively well-off, and they are politically active. We predict that these characteristics will become increasingly salient by the year 2000.

A vigorous and educated young-old group can be expected to develop new needs with regard to the meaningful use of time. They will want a wide range of options and opportunities both for self-enhancement and for community participation.

With regard to work, some will opt for early retirement; some will want to continue to work beyond 65; some will want to undertake new work careers at one or more times after age 40. The young-old are likely to encourage economic policies that hasten the separation between income and work, with the goal of providing retirees with sufficient income to approximate their pre-retirement living standards.

We are already seeing a trend which will probably accelerate: a wider range of life patterns with regard to work, education, and leisure. More middle-aged and older people are seeking education, some because of obsolescence of work skills, others for recreation or self-fulfillment. Plans are now in progress in various parts of the country to create intergenerational campuses, and in this and other ways to help bring into reality the so-called "learning society."

The needs of the young-old in housing, location, and transportation will be increasingly affected by the decisions they make with regard to the use of leisure time. The desire to find interesting things to do will lead them to seek environments which will maximize options for meaningful pursuits. If opportunities are provided for meaningful community participation in their present communities, fewer rather than more are likely to move to age-segregated retirement communities.

The young-old are likely to want greater options for what generally might be called an "age-irrelevant" society, one in which arbitrary constraints based on chronological age are removed, and in which all individuals have opportunities consonant with their needs, desires, and abilities, whether they be young or old.

Over-all, as the young-old articulate their needs and desires, the emphasis is likely to be upon improving the quality of life and upon increasing the choices of life styles.

The Old-Old

The visibility of the young-old is not to denigrate the old-old, nor to neglect their needs. An increasing minority of the old-old will remain active and productive and, because this is true, will want increased options in all areas of life. The majority will probably live independently, but many will need supportive social services, or home health services, or special features in the physical environment to enable them to function as fully as possible. Without taking an overly optimistic view, it is likely that such services will grow, and that they will become more effective not only in slowing physical and mental deterioration, but in preventing unnecessary decline in feelings of self-worth and dignity.

There is no denying the fact that at the very end of life there will be a shorter or longer period of dependency, nor that there will be increased numbers of the old-old who will need special care, either in their own homes or in institutional settings. New and difficult ethical questions will arise regarding what share of the health and services budget of the nation should go to the old-old. For persons who are terminally ill or incapacitated, the problems for the society will continue to be how to provide the maximum care and comfort, the assurance of dignified death, but also how to provide a greater element of choice for the individual himself or for members of his family regarding how and when his life shall end. The future will probably see the spread of educational programs aimed at the public at large as well as at various professional groups for achieving a "best death" for each individual.

The Future Roles of the Young-Old

To turn now to the broader question of the relation between age groups and how they may change in the future, older persons will probably continue to move away from the roles of economic producer and increasingly become the users of leisure time. In those new roles, the young-old may be the first age group to reach the society of the future. How will they experiment with what some observers would call the truly human condition—the condition of freedom from work and freedom from want?

With their relative good health, education, purchasing power, free time, and political involvement, they are not likely to become neglected members of the society. Will they, instead, become social contributors? Will they create new service roles with or without financial remuneration?

Will they become major agents of social change in building an age-irrelevant society? If they create an attractive image of aging and thus allay the fears of the young about growing old, they will play a significant role in shaping the society of the future.

References

Carnegie Commission on Higher Education, *Toward a Learning Society*. New York: McGraw-Hill, 1973.

Comfort, A. Longer life by 1990? *New Scientist*, Dec., 1959, 549–551.

Johnston, D. F. The future of work: Three possible alternatives. *Monthly Labor Review*, May 1972. United States Department of Labor: Washington, D.C.

Neugarten, B. L. Age groups in American society and the rise of the young-old. *Annals of the American Academy of Political & Social Science*, Sept., 1974, 187–198.

Shanas, E., Townsend, P., Wedderburn, D., Friis, H., Milhoj, P., & Stehouwer, J. *Old People in Three Industrial Societies*, New York: Atherton Press, 1968.

Strehler, B. Ten myths about aging. *Center Magazine*, July, 1970, 41–48.

Verba, S., & Nie, N. H. *Participation in America*. New York: Harper and Row, 1972.

11

DESIGNS FOR LIVING

ROSLYN LINDHEIM

The environments that will be built for the elderly at the end of this century and beyond will depend on our political, economic, social, technological, and human goals. The man-made environment, whether it is buildings, communities, or cities, mirrors the nature of our institutions and the priorities of the decision makers. In particular, design of environments for the elderly reflects the way in which we see the róle of old people in our society. Because buildings say so much about reality, we can reconstruct the nature of a society from its architecture. Our present and future communities are the living archeology from which we can extract, without pretense and verbiage, the actual values held by our society. Thus, if we say we care for old people and then build buildings which isolate them from the rest of the community and stuff them into holes for dying, the facts contradict the words. Looking at the design of environments for the elderly circa 2000 in a concentrated technological view leads us to a further Orwellian horror.

The key question is where do we want to put our resources for the aged—into medicine, buildings, services, production, enjoyment? Decisions such as these will drastically affect the type of facility we build and determine what we mean by future-oriented living. In order to develop viable communities, the term "design" must have a broader meaning than physical design. According to Webster's Dictionary, design is "the deliberate, purposeful planning of a settled coherent program for selecting the means and contriving the elements, steps and procedures which will adequately satisfy some need." Therefore, the quality of the environments of 2000 and beyond will be determined by our success or failure in redirecting our priorities today. The issue is not what will be here 20 years hence but what we do now and in the immediate years to come.

There is probably no aspect of the physical environment where goals are more ambiguous than in the design of facilities for the aged. The issues involved reflect society's approach to youth and age, life and death, sickness and health. The questions posed are primarily ethical, cultural, and economic, not architectural. Paradoxically, the achievements of urbanization, modern technology, and medical advance have created their own Frankensteins. As life expectancy increases, so does disease and disability. The technology which has allowed for the development of our cities has also produced the pollution and accidents which render them dangerous. As transportation and communication created the possibilities of linking people together, increased mobility and patterns of living isolated families from one another. The efficiency which is required for industrial productivity has exiled large sections of the population from being a part of the productive process. Moreover, the nature of disease reflects this changing nature of our lives.

On the occasion of his Congressional Award, Jonas Salk (1965) observed in an address that: ". . . man himself is now bringing about vast and rapid changes in his environment and is therefore producing an effect in which it is the environment created by him rather than the environment of nature, that exerts a dominant influence upon his evolutionary history . . . the transformation that is taking place is a shift from mainly physical diseases to social illnesses."

In a talk before the American Association of Homes for the Aged, the late Dr. E. Richard Weinerman of Yale University said, in discussing modern environmental problems of the aged:

> . . . the very nature of disease has changed to a pattern in which chronicity, long-term interference with usual life skills, and complex dysfunction are the common characteristics, particularly for the elderly. The traditional model of disease, in which the state of health is suddenly disrupted by an acute and specific disorder, to end dramatically in recovery or death, no longer applies. . . . The picture now is that of multiple environmental (man-made) causative factors, insidious onset, derangements of many different systems which fail to fit neatly into diagnostic pigeonholes—increasing disabilities despite powerful modern therapies. (1966, p. 965)

Lifestyles have also changed with urbanization. There has been a shift, particularly in the care of the infirm aged, from the family environment to that of hospitals and nursing homes. Even two generations ago people died in their own beds, theoretically, at least, in the bosom of their families. Today, of the people who die of old age and chronic disease, half die in hospitals and a third die in nursing homes or old peoples' homes. We have not yet found a way to give dignity and serenity to the last years of life, either economically, financially, socially, or architecturally. This is a serious problem which affects not only the old but the young as well.

The institutions we provide for those who cannot care for themselves are human garbage heaps—a result of and a reinforcement of our tendency to avoid confronting social and interpersonal problems. In *The Pursuit of Loneliness*, Philip Slater (1970) writes:

Our ideas about institutionalizing the aged, psychotic, retarded and infirm are based on a pattern of thought that we might call the Toilet Assumption—the notion that unwanted matter, unwanted difficulties, unwanted complexities and obstacles will disappear if they are removed from our immediate field of vision. . . . We throw the aged and psychotic into institutional holes where they cannot be seen. Our approach to social problems is to decrease their visibility: out of sight, out of mind. . . . The result of our social efforts has been to remove the underlying problems of our society farther and farther from the daily experience and daily consciousness, and hence to decrease in the mass of the population, the knowledge, skill, resources, and motivation necessary to deal with it. (p. 15).

My work as an architect would be akin to prostitution if I researched and then built better leisure worlds when I believe the need is work instead of leisure; or created better designs for segregated communities when I believe the wholeness of life depends on integration; or planned more humane nursing homes when I know they are death houses; or established new environments for death when I believe death must be integrally related to life.

Therefore, before settling for design environments which ostracize the elderly from society, let us reexamine some of the needs for life which affect the well-being of both young and old and see in what manner the physical environment can serve as a reinforcing system to enable people to meet them most effectively. I see as basic:

1. The need to be socially useful
2. The need to exercise choice as to where and how one lives while still maintaining continuity and roots
3. The need to be cared for when one is sick and feeble
4. The need, indeed the right, for death to be treated not as an illness but as a natural process of life

The Need to be Socially Useful

Eric Fromm has said that old age is a problem created by modern industrial society. In his view, the aged are a problem because they are superconsumers of time in a society which values productive work (Fromm, 1966). In the United States, the most highly valued role is work, and productivity is the primary measure of role performance. As one progresses through the life cycle, numerous role alternatives are available until age 65. However, at 65, work-role alternatives disappear for the majority of individuals. It is at this age that individuals are regarded as less productive and required to abandon work-roles in favor of more youthful members of society. Since productivity is crucial for both survival and social acceptance, those over 65 are frequently viewed as social liabilities and they are excluded from the most highly valued role (Bruhn, 1971).

Yet, in studies of satisfaction and dissatisfaction, there is evidence that elderly people who do work derive greater satisfaction from their work than from leisure activities. In an article on the use of leisure time, Eric Pfeiffer and Glenn C. Davis (1971) have shown that of the elderly subjects interviewed, more than half indicated that this was true and they would still work even if they did not have to.

In his classic article, "Old Age: One Moral Dilemma of an Affluent Society," Irving Rosow (1962) points out that in pre-industrial societies the relative welfare of the old person in his group improves:

> . . . to the extent that the productivity of the economy is low and the need for labor creates opportunities and functions for older people . . . that America does not rate high on those factors which reinforce the position of old people in less advanced societies. Paradoxically, our productivity is too high and our mutual dependence too low. We are too wealthy as a nation and economically too self-sufficient as individuals to need the old person. Hence, his position is not reinforced by pressing social functions which he can perform. (p. 184).

In such areas as the Caucasus, where there are many aged, the old people continue to be contributing, productive members of their society. The economy is agrarian, there is no fixed retirement age, and the elderly make themselves useful doing many tasks around the farm or in the home (Leaf, 1973).

Environments that are especially designed for the well-to-do are characterized by consumption. Even their names connote vacation, country, leisure: Sun City, The Sequoias, Leisure World, Retirement Village. Sun City boasts six golf courses to serve as many as 2,500 golfers at once. The Del Webb Company expects Sun City to double in population to 55,000 by 1980. In a series of interviews of residents of Sun City, it was apparent that busy-work was the order of the day. As one resident said, "How many ash trays do you have to make to feel worthwhile? How many games of bridge do you have to play?" (Lancaster, 1972). People keep coming, however, for whatever diversions Sun City has to offer are better than nothing at all. Sun City represents wealthy consumerism, as do Palm Springs, Miami, and Rossmoor. The poor consumer can be found in old hotels, rooming houses, and skid rows.

An integral part of "future-oriented design" must be opportunities for work, not busywork, but productive work in the deepest sense, so that people will be able, despite their years, to participate to their maximum capacity. Viable work opportunities for the elderly would require standards of productivity based on a person's capabilities rather than on prescribed notions of efficiency. This in turn would allow for changes in the scale of operation, the location of work places, and their environmental contexts. It is interesting to note that industry was started on the kibbutz in Israel to provide work for the older inhabitants who could no longer work in the fields.

On the occasion of his 90th birthday, the great black scholar, W. E. B. Dubois (1968) said to his great-grandson, "As men go, I have had a reasonably happy and successful life. I have had enough to eat and drink, have been suitably clothed and, as you see, have had many friends. But the thing which has been the secret of whatever I have done is the fact that I have been able to earn a living by doing the work which I wanted to do and work which the world needed done" (p. 398). He continued working until he died at 93.

The Need to Exercise Choice as to Where and How One Lives While Still Maintaining Continuity and Roots

The aged are just like everyone else, only older. There are just as diverse personalities, backgrounds, lifestyles, and preferences among the elderly as in any other age group. And just as there is no one way to meet the needs of any group of people, there is no one way to prescribe for the elderly. There are old-old people and young-old people, married and single, healthy and sick, wealthy and poor. Within each of these groupings there are infinite varieties and combinations of personalities and preferences, ways in which to contribute to society and to one's own self-actualization. Perhaps the most crucial consideration for the life and wellbeing of the elderly is the power to grow old without uprooting oneself from family, friends, and familiar surroundings; and within these parameters to have a number of choices about how and where one lives. There is no such thing as an ideal environment; there are, instead, different fits between individual needs and specific environmental conditions. The problems are threefold: how to provide sufficient resources for the individual so that he or she can genuinely have a choice about how and where to live; how to provide different "sets" of solutions for problems, rather than only one way; and how to provide the diversity required to meet the changing needs of the elderly within a given geographical area so that family ties and friendships can be maintained.

To date, most environmental research has concentrated on housing types, access to health and social services, parks, and transportation. I believe that special emphasis should be placed on how to design a city that supports, rather than negates, the concept of intergenerational family relationships. Some work has been done on living arrangements for two- and three-generation occupance, second homes on large lots, legislation to enable older home owners to keep their homes and remodel them if necessary for more income or greater convenience, and shifts in zoning to allow for intermingling of work, living, nursing homes, or recreation.

Of course, I am for barrier-free architecture, but I find that greater than any physical barriers are the barriers between people caused by the fear of developing a dependence upon one another. Philip Slater (1970) says, "One of the major goals of technology in America is to free us from the necessity of relating to, submitting to, depending upon or controlling other people. Unfortunately, the more we have succeeded in doing this the more we have felt disconnected, bored, lonely, unprotected, unnecessary and unsafe" (p. 26).

The Need to be Cared for When One is Sick and Feeble

It is certain that in the 21st century many elderly who cannot adequately take care of themselves will need supportive elements. To date, our institutional arrangements for caring for the elderly—old age homes, nursing homes, and leaving them to die in hospitals—are appalling, particularly when matched against our supposed resources.

Simone de Beauvoir (1972) describes old age institutions in France with devastating vividness:

About 178,000 hospital or institution beds are housed in buildings a
hundred years old. These are often former hospitals, castles, barracks
or prisons that are in no way suited to their new functions. They have a
great many staircases and no lifts, so that some old people cannot leave
their floor. Dormitories were condemned in 1958, but in fact, the great
majority of beds are so arranged, and in these beds the sick and
bedridden lie all day long. Often there is no screen between beds, no
private bed table, no private locker. The old person does not possess an
inch of space he can call his own. Figures show that of the healthy old
people admitted to such an institution, 8 percent die in the first week,
28.7 percent die in the first month, 45 percent die in the first six
months, 54.4 percent die in the first year, and 64.4 percent die in the
first two years. (pp. 255 & 256).

de Beauvoir further states:

More than half the old people die within a year of their admission. It is
not only the living conditions in an institution that are responsible: with
the aged, any kind of uprooting may cause death. It is, rather, the fate
of those who survive that should be deplored. In a great number of
cases this fate may be summed up in a few words—abandonment,
segregation, decay, dementia, death. (p. 256).

In the United States there is a numbness about the
design of nursing homes. We think if they look nice from
the outside, if the lobby has carpeting, if there are two in a
room instead of many, the situation is better. It is only a
little better, and we should not let our senses be lulled by
such externals. The therapeutic value of the "home" environment is constantly referred to by doctors, sociologists,
and gerontologists. They will invariably say, "make it home-
like," when discussing the architectural design of a hospital
or nursing home. The architectural results, particularly
with respect to the newer and larger nursing homes, are
double corridor scheme modeled after the acute nursing
unit of a hospital, but with chintz curtains, pictures on the
wall, and a recreation room.

Home in the genuine sense means warmth and love

and contact with others on an intimate basis. It also means the exercise of choice, in that every day we make frequent choices in minor matters, and so exercise our preference for different sorts of food, clothing, entertainment, and to some extent, for the company of other people. A large family living in a home rarely contains more than eight persons and includes different generations and different sexes.

In contrast to the home environment, hospitals and nursing homes are places where living, working, and recreation occur in one physical location. There is little room for individuality of expression by differences in dress or personal possessions. The types of choices made in everyday living are restricted. Sick and lonely people are sometimes placed in single rooms or two in a room, on the assumption that privacy is good, or at other times, placed in large wards with no privacy at all. Because there is an understanding of the need for a change of place, a large recreation room is provided for everybody, usually at the end of a long corridor, for the purpose of allowing patients to interact with each other.

This compulsory interaction with so many other sick people results most often in the patient's retiring psychologically into his or her own shell, or, in contrast, acting out against the environment. People in institutions live communally with a minimum of privacy; their relationships with each other, however, are slender. Many subsist in a kind of defensive isolationism with mobility restricted and little access to general society (Osmond, 1970).

Perhaps elderly people's greatest need is for contact with outside society. Those who require extended care, whatever the variety of physical or mental disability, have a harder time sustaining contacts with other people. In their normal lives they would have a multitude of physical, auditory, visual, and written contact. It is necessary, therefore, for persons within an institution to be able to maintain contact with friends and relatives as well as to seek meaningful contact with others within the institution.

Dehumanizing elements programmed into the design of nursing homes do not come from some deliberate decision as to "we shall or shall not humanize" but stem rather inevitably from the way we weigh our total value system in this society, giving priority to economy, productivity, and efficiency. In terms of well-being and care for the individual, these criteria may actually be neither efficient, economical, nor productive.

Death Should be Treated as a Natural Process, Not as an Illness

I mentioned earlier that half the people today die in hospitals and another third die in homes for the aged. America's way of life insulates us from death and dying. In their book, *The Psychology of Death*, Robert Kastenbaum and Ruth Aisenberg (1972) describe how illness and death are removed from household management and how even within hospital walls, the patient is not supposed to die in just any place at any time. It is deemed important that the survivors (other patients, staff, visitors) not be exposed to the phenomena of death except under carefully specified circumstances. The staff is angry when death occurs in the wrong place.

Robert Blauner (1969), in his article "Death and Social Structure," writes that "in premodern societies, many deaths take place amid the hubbub of life, in the central territory of the tribe, clan or other familial group. In modern societies, where the majority of deaths are now predictable in the older age brackets, disengagement from family and economic function has permitted the segregation of death settings from more workaday social territory." Two recent sociological studies show the attutides within the hospital toward the dying patient and the essential loneliness of a hospital death (Glaser & Strauss, 1968). In general, patients die in the hospital either in the super-technological environment of intensive coronary care or, in an effort to minimize the disturbance for others, are isolated in a private room to die alone. Isolation of death from the natural processes of life has a drastic effect on the way we design for the elderly. If death occurs outside the home and is only associated with the old, the sick, and takes place in institutions, then these institutions, no matter how you look at them, are death houses.

If death and aging are to be reassociated with life and its natural processes, then life must once again be exposed to death. The architectural paradigms which govern nursing homes, hospitals, and even Sun Cities ask how to hide death, where to put it, how to sneak the body away. In this process, we also sneak the elderly away from life.

In the book *Triage* (Lewin, 1972), which I hope is fiction, there is a description of a systematic program to reduce the population in order to provide sufficient resources for those in power. As a method of eliminating the population, there are increasing numbers of deaths in nursing homes because of fires, food poisoning, gas leaks, accidents, etc. However, nobody thinks to investigate the cause of these deaths—first, because nobody cares and second because it is all so far away from our lives.

Ivan Illich (1977) has written a brilliant chapter, "Death against Death," in which he shows how the ritual nature of modern health procedures hides from doctors and patients the contradiction between the ideal of a natural death and the reality of the clinical death in which most people's lives now actually end. Our vulnerability in the face of death, and its physical location away from where we live our lives, has stripped us of the ability to deal with it in a dignified manner as a natural process of life. Death at home must be recognized. Such new institutions as the hospices outside London, of which St. Christopher's is the best known, must be incorporated as integral parts of communities. They provide an environment which recognizes the social and physical needs of the dying patient for understanding and care as well as for relief from pain. In addition, hospices sometimes serve as centers for home-care programs which help families tend the dying patient at home (Morison, 1973). The hiding of death has taken away our ability to deal with it.

Conclusion

The key problems in building future environments for the elderly are learning how to plan our lives so that there is an opportunity for intergenerational living and dying, and for finding work opportunities—with play and recreation interspersed—so that access, supervision, and interdependence become a way of life. Irving Rosow (1962) ably stated:

> By now, it should be clear that the crucial people in the aging problem are not the old, but the younger age groups; it is the rest of us who determine the status and position of the old person in the social order. What is at stake for the future is not only the alienation of the old from the young, but the alienation of the young from each other and of man from man. There is no real way out of this dilemma for young or old without a basic re-ordering of our national aspirations and values, of which the aging problem is but a token. Anything less than this will see us concentrating only on superficial systems, especially tangible ones like housing the aged, and nibbling at the tattered edges of our problems without penetrating to their heart. (p. 191).

If we are serious about looking toward future-oriented design for the 21st century and beyond, we cannot settle for discovering how to design better concentration camps for the elderly, either now or then.

> A Man's work, however finished it seems,
> Continues as long as he lives.
> A man, however perfect he seems,
> Is needed as long as he lives.
>
> Lao Tzu

References

Blauner, R. Death and social structure. In Rose Laub Coser (Ed.), *Life Cycle and Achievement in America*. New York: Harper Torchbooks, 1969.

Bruhn, J. G. An ecological perspective of aging. *The Gerontologist*, 1971, *II* (3), 187–195.

De Beauvoir, S. *The coming of age*. New York: G. P. Putnam, 1972.

Du Bois, W. E. B. *Autobiography*. New York: International Publishers, 1968.

Fromm, E. Psychological problems of aging. *Journal of Rehabilitation*, 1966, *32*, 10–12.

Glaser, B. G., & Strauss, A. L. Temporal aspects of dying as a non-scheduled status passage. In Bernice Neugarten (Ed.), *Middle age and aging: A reader in social psychology.* Chicago: University of Chicago Press, 1968.

Illich, I. Death against death. In *Medical Nemesis: The Expropriation of Health.* New York: Bantam, 1977.

Kastenbaum, R., & Aisenberg, R. *The Psychology of Death.* New York: Springer Company, 1972.

Lancaster, H. The old but affluent withdraw to Sun City to fill empty days. *Wall Street Journal,* November 17, 1972.

Leaf, A. Getting old. *Scientific American,* 1973, *229* (3), 44–52.

Lewin, L. C. *Triage.* New York: Warner Books, 1972.

Morison, R. S. Dying. *Scientific American,* 1973, *229* (3), 54.

Osmond, H. Function as the basis of psychiatric need design. In *Environment Psychology: Man and his Physical Setting.* H. Proshansky, W. H. Ittelson, & L. G. Rivlin (Eds.) New York: Holt, Rinehart & Winston, 1970.

Pfeiffer, E. & Davis, G. C. The use of leisure time in middle life. *The Gerontologist,* 1971, *2* (3), 187–195.

Rosow, I. Old age: One moral dilemma of an affluent society. *The Gerontologist,* 1962, *2* (4), 182–191.

Salk, J. E. Address on the occasion of receipt of Congressional Award. *New York Times,* April 13, 1965.

Slater, P. *The Pursuit of Loneliness: American Culture at the Breaking Point.* Boston: Beacon Press, 1970.

Weinerman, E. R. The role of the interdisciplinary team. In *The Social Components of Care.* New York: American Association of Homes for the Aging. 1966.

Reference Notes

1. Osmond, H. Hospitals for the mentally ill. (Mimeographed paper) University of Saskatchewan, Saskatoon, 1976.

12

DESIGNS FOR LEARNING

HOWARD Y. McCLUSKY

Before looking ahead to the year 2000 and beyond, I would like to begin this discussion by looking back to the summer of 1970. At that time I was completing a Background Paper on Education for the 1971 White House Conference on Aging. I was fortunate in having access to the counsel of an Advisory Committee composed of distinguished leaders in the field. With the aid of two research assistants we scoured the gerontological and educational domains for statements of policy and reports of practice related to education and aging. Except for a few scattered programs operating at the local level we drew a blank.

At the national level, neither the United States Office of Education and the Administration on Aging, representing the governmental sector, nor the American Council on Education and the National Association of Public Continuing and Adult Education, representing the private sector, had anything to offer. One refreshing exception was the Adult Education Association of the United States' section on aging, sponsored since the 1950s. Even here the involvement was minimal.

At the state level the picture was no better. State Commissions on Aging gave little if any attention to education per se, and New York was the only state with a section on Aging in its Department of Education.

At the same time the results of research indicated that rates of participation in educational activities were lower for the elderly than for any age segment of the population, a condition reflected in the fact that the 1970 Handbook of Adult Education, the most widely consulted reference in the field, had no room for the subject of Education for Aging within its pages.

In brief, in the summer of 1970, education for aging was distinguished for occupying the lowest rank in the priorities of both the gerontological and educational establishments. It was the "orphan in the attic of the stepchild."

I report this bleak picture of almost total neglect in order to establish a contrast to the wholly different situation I predict will prevail in the year 2000 and beyond. By 2000, education for lifelong learning will have become thoroughly accepted in policy and well on its way to implementation in practice. Emphasis on the adult dimension of lifelong learning will be having, by the year 2000, a profound impact on both the opportunities and the character of education of persons at all age levels. Thus programs of education for aging will constitute the culminating phase of a much more comprehensive movement. It will be the crest on a much larger wave. Therefore, in order to understand and anticipate the years ahead we must place the prospects for education for aging in the perspective of a larger context, that is, the context of an expanding demand for a participation in programs of adult education at all stages of adult life.

Let us briefly examine some of the factors that have led us to make this prediction. First, adult schedules will contain more nonwork time for discretionary use. Earlier retirement ("30 and out") and the shorter work week are illustrative of this trend. Second, education will become an increasingly important component of the job itself. On the job training, the "blue collar sabbatical," " recurrent education" are again illustrative.

Third, there will be a growing number of persons in the adult population who take part in continuing education. For instance, it is well established that the higher the level of a person's formal education the greater the likelihood that he or she will return to some form of instruction in the years thereafter. A few years ago the average level of formal schooling in the United States was the ninth grade; in 1976 it is approaching the 12th grade; by 2000 it will approximate the 14th grade.

Fourth, the factor that will have the most decisive impact on education in the years ahead is that of societal change. There is no evidence that the rate of change which has strongly dominated the third quarter of the 20th century will have subsided by the year 2000. On the contrary, change will continue to occur so rapidly and the impact will continue to be so pervasive that all aspects of living will be increasingly subjected to processes of ongoing transformation; hence the demand for continuing education. The alternative will be deterioration for both individual and society into obsolescence. By the year 2000, the myth that a person can learn enough in 12, 14, 16 or more years of schooling to last a lifetime, and collaterally that childhood and youth is the period in which learning can best take place, will have become thoroughly exploded. It will be replaced with the belief that participation in continuing education is appropriate adult behavior and that some of the most significant learning of the entire lifespan can occur in the later years.

At the same time equally significant developments will be taking place in the domain of gerontology. By the year 2000, the private sector serving the elderly will be more firmly established, will be managed by more professionally trained personnel, and will be conducting programs more responsive to the needs of their clientele. Included in this category of effort will be such agencies as churches, senior centers, libraries, financial institutions, recreational associations, and health clinics.

A similar prediction can be made for the public sector. The functions of state offices on aging will be more clearly defined and their major activities established well beyond the stage of field testing. Moreover, if we can judge from the first three years of its existence, and if we can use the history of the Cooperative Extension Service of the United States Department of Agriculture as a rough parallel, the area agencies of the Administration on Aging should, by the year 2000, constitute a highly effective administrative vehicle for serving the needs of the elderly even in the most remote community of the country.

Most important, however, is the well-known fact that by 2000 there will be both absolutely and relatively more persons in the population past 65. They will be more financially secure, healthier, and better educated; have higher expectations; be better organized; be served by more sophisticated leadership; and possess more political clout.

To summarize, by the year 2000 the fields of both adult education and gerontology will be experiencing a stage of dynamic development. Adult education will have moved from the margin to the center of educational practice and the elderly, with a growing number of influential spokesmen, reinforced by the pressures of a growing societal concern, will be in a better position to claim their share of educational resources. The climate will have become extremely favorable for the development of a wide range of programs in a diverse assortment of agencies.

At this point we will examine these developments under two categories of effort. One will consist of activities accenting the educational dimension of gerontology and the other will consist of programs emphasizing the gerontological dimension of education.

In the first category, let us look at the areas of (a) "congregate living" and (b) program services.

By the year 2000 we will regard situations of "congregate living," such as nursing homes and housing for seniors, as offering the potential of becoming educative communities. Living within a fairly limited geographical area, residents will constitute an accessible and identifiable population from which an audience for educational purposes may be recruited. Also, proximitous living will provide an opportunity for residents to engage in educative dialogue about common interests, concerns, and aspirations. Situations of "congregate living" will also lend themselves to the use of decentralized instruction. By the year

2000 there will be significant advances in the use of mobile teaching units, "talking books," independent study, the telephone, two-way television and radio, etc. As a result of such advantages, nursing homes will be regarded not only as custodial but also as educational in character; and residential centers will be viewed not only as low-cost housing but also as campuses for diverse instructional programs.

This will require a reconceptualization of the role of "congregate living" for the elderly and a new approach to recruiting and training personnel necessary for the implementation of this role. The stimulus value óf the total primary face-to-face environment will be assessed in the light of its educative potential.

A second opportunity for education is contained in programs of services for the elderly. It is assumed that such service is performed in response to a vital need, or a lack or deprivation; that the elderly person is "hurting," and in extreme cases his or her survival may be at stake. Examples of services set up to meet such needs are nursing care, "meals on wheels," legal counsel, assistance with the computation of income taxes, and advice on housing.

All these and similar instances constitute situations in which elderly persons are highly involved. The value of these situations as "arousal stimuli" is formidable. They are what the educator calls "teachable moments" and if viewed as such, present exceptionally provocative opportunities for instruction. This instruction may be ad hoc in character and require nontraditional styles of teaching, but it can contribute impressively to the ability of the elderly person to cope effectively with the demands of his or her environment. For example, a low-cost meal at a Senior Center may not only provide food for the body but also an occasion for instruction in good nutrition. A diagnostic medical examination may not only yield important information about the state of elderly person's physical condition but also provide an opportunity to instruct the client in effective measures for the maintenance of health.

In brief, we are predicting that the exploitation of the educational opportunities of congregate living and program services will, by 2000, contribute a totally new set of components to the environment in which the elderly are compelled to live, providing more functional skills for solving problems with which they are forced to cope. Because education will come to the client, it will help overcome the barriers that arise from difficulties of transportation and will also meet the needs of the hidden, difficult to reach elderly person, often bypassed by conventional formats of instruction. This could be the first step inducing the underparticipant elderly to take part in more systematic and formal programs of inquiry.

We will turn now to a discussion of the second category of educational developments that will be well underway by the year 2000; namely, those involving an expansion of the gerontological dimension of the educational enterprise.

Let us now examine what is likely to occur in the systems of informal education. There is every reason to believe that informal, noncredential agencies of education will continue to constitute a major vehicle for education of the elderly. The mandate of these agencies to serve the elderly, however, will be more explicit; support for providing this service will be more secure; and personnel will be better trained. Senior centers will be more likely to expand educational programs along with the traditional recreational focus of the center movement. Public libraries will be collecting more materials especially designed to meet the requirements of the elderly. Libraries will also be more "outreaching" in orientation and heavily committed to delivering their services by mobile units and staff to locations where the elderly live. Churches will also develop programs more explicitly designed for the service to the elderly, both unilaterally and via coalitions. The Home-Making Division of the Cooperative Extension Service will have slanted its long-established programs in nutrition, consumer education, and family living to serve the elderly and, beginning with its First National Conference on Aging, held in September, 1976, will have given services to the elderly much higher priority in both policy and practice. Similar predictions can be made for the media, banks, centers for consumer education, health clinics, etc.

This brings us to a consideration of the role of the system of formal education in developing programs in education for aging. We predict that practically every institution of higher learning in the United States will have established comprehensive programs of instruction and research in the field of gerontology by the year 2000. They will continue to be interdisciplinary in character.

The mission of higher education will be twofold; it will train professional workers and gerontologize general education. Both colleges and universities will be heavily engaged in preparing students for research and teaching in gerontology at both pre- and post-secondary levels of instruction. At the same time they will also be training personnel required to staff the growing number of service programs operated by public and private agencies.

In the second instance, higher education will develop the subject matter of gerontology as part of nonvocational general liberal education. This will be accomplished by "curricular infiltration"; a gerontological component will become a part of most departments of academic inquiry. We base this prediction on the premise that, by the year 2000, as part of growing societal awareness, the young, middle-aged, and elderly will recognize the importance of understanding gerontological phenomena as a prerequisite for comprehending the meaning of human development.

Understandably, programs of training for professional workers will for the most part attract young persons in the process of starting careers and middle-aged persons engaged in shifting careers. However, training programs could also appeal to a substantial number of the elderly seeking to establish themselves in part- or full-time second careers.

We predict, however, that programs of general education, with or without the "gerontological component," will appeal to a much larger number of the elderly. They will be welcomed by both colleges and universities in order to fill vacancies caused by a decrease in enrollment of students of traditional college age. Moreover, because of their higher levels of formal education they will, as indicated at the outset of this chapter, be more likely to be the kinds of persons who return to participation in higher education.

Most significant for our argument, however, is the fact that, by the year 2000, a growing number of colleges and universities will be developing programs designed especially for the elderly. This could include an expansion of projects already in existence and flourishing (1976), such as the Donovan Scholars program at the University of Kentucky and the intergenerational programs at Fairhaven College in Washington, Bucknell University in Pennsylvania, and St. Benedict's College in Minnesota, as well as the Institute of Retired Professionals in New York City. Also included could be the plans of some colleges and universities to establish model residential projects for retirees in order to facilitate their participation in academic offerings and their assistance in conducting research in the field.

The third quarter of the 20th century witnessed two of the most significant developments in the history of American education—the community college and the community school. Together they constitute a network of operational structures capable of delivering programs of educational services to the most remote residents they are authorized to serve. We must give high priority to the contributive potential of these two educational agencies in education for aging.

Perhaps the most distinguishing feature of the community school and the community college is their thorough commitment to the educational service of "ALL persons of ALL ages at ALL times." It is not surprising, therefore, that some of the most innovative and effective programs of education about and for the elderly have taken place under their sponsorship. Within the boundaries of their respective domains, each institution has its own unique pattern of strength. Substantively, the community college excels in providing a wide array of instructional services. A case in point is its training of professional workers and general education. By contrast, the neighborhood community school, within walking distance of the elementary school pupil, is much closer to where the elderly actually live and thus overcomes the barriers of communication and transportation which prevent many elderly from taking part in educational programs.

Because these two institutions have become solidly established as a matter of national policy and are receiving increased legislative support at local, state, and national levels, there is every reason to believe that their contribution to education for and about aging will, by the year 2000, be massive. In terms of number of persons served and the relevance of programs developed, their contributive potential, amply demonstrated, is one of the reasons for viewing the future of education for and about aging with optimism.

This brings us to some concluding speculations about the future of selected substantive aspects of the field.

First, because of the changing position of women in modern society and especially when we add the fact that women live longer and hence outnumber men in the later years, a strong case can be made for designing programs for both pre- and postretirement education explicitly directed at meeting the unique needs of women for autonomy and independence. Typically, the field of retirement education has been developed to buffer the adjustment of men as they withdraw from the labor force. In the future this field of instruction must and will be reconceptualized to include the equally authentic and special requirements of women.

Second, by the year 2000 occupational training for the elderly will receive much more attention than it has received since the advent of mandatory retirement. This prediction is based on the following considerations:

1. The number of persons in the productive years of life, that is, 20 to 60, will be smaller and thereby encourage a return of the elderly to the labor force in order to share the burden of providing funds for Social Security.

2. More roles for the performance of the elderly will have been discovered for which they are uniquely adapted and for which some training will be relevant, if not necessary.

3. There is a strong possibility that the regulations now governing mandatory retirement will have become modified so as to encourage a partial return of the elderly to productive employment.

Third, by the year 2000 the elderly will be better organized, be served by more sophisticated leadership, and possess more political clout than they do at present. This could lead to a dramatic redistribution of political power in the United States and will call for a type of citizenship transcending that which currently prevails. If this power should materialize, it would be disastrous for the society if it were devoted exclusively to securing more privileges for the elderly. If the elderly are destined to become powerful, then education aimed at cultivating their statesman and service roles will become imperative. It will require a fresh conceptualization of what the "elderly as citizen" can and should be and a renewed commitment by agencies of adult education to see that this conceptualization is translated into practice.

We predict that the most fundamental development that will take place by 2000 will be the recognition of the importance of the quality of life in the later years as a basis for providing an integrative standard for shaping the character of earlier education in the earlier years. In other words, we are proposing that in the future, life in the later years will, at its culminating best, serve as a guide for education in all years and stages of development.

Several outcomes would result from an acceptance and implementation of this proposition. It would mean that education for and about aging would begin in the elementary school and continue throughout life. It would emphasize the importance of childhood and youth education, laying the foundations for successful living in the later years. It would provide valid criteria for determining priorities in curriculum development. To be more generic, it would make use of the concept of the "spiral curriculum" in the timing of instruction. Ideas, themes, and facts of supreme importance for life at its culminating best would be introduced early in a student's educational career and reintroduced at successive levels of maturity appropriate for the developmental stage of the person involved. To illustrate: since good health is perhaps the most important requirement for the enjoyment of the later years, instruction aimed at producing good health in childhood, youth, and the years thereafter would become supremely important. The economics, compensatory skills, human relations, etc., undergirding life at its culminating best would also provide subject matter.

The preceding paragraphs constitute only the bare bones of what the impact may be on the educational practice of a perspective derived from life in the later years. We are not arguing that this criterion will be fully accepted by the year 2000, but we do believe that some development in its direction will be well underway and that its ultimate acceptance will be brought about by forces that are already in operation and give promise of continuing influence in the years ahead.

Why do we take this stand? Because we believe that society cannot afford to be burdened with the albatross of a growing mass of dependent elderly persons. However, the conscience of society will demand that the elderly have adequate opportunities for living with self respect and dignity.

Society will need models of successful living in the later years as a guide for personal development and as a means for giving younger persons a positive image of their own future. Society will need to comprehend life in its completeness in order to place any stage of development in lifespan perspective. As a guide for the validation and attainment of the above, we will need the ideal of life at its culminating best.

Conclusion

Any attempt to anticipate the future of any phenomenon is inevitably overshadowed with uncertainty and must necessarily be highly speculative in character. As a result the preceding discussion is a blend of what we have regarded to be feasible, probable, possible, and "oughtable." In spite of its fragile base in hard data, practically every prediction we have ventured is an extrapolation of trends that are already underway and the reflection of events that have occurred in the past six years. In our judgment, these events are not instances of fads that will have their day and soon pass away but are the outcome of forces that will continue to operate and possibly gain in momentum in the years ahead. In brief, we believe that the future of education for and about aging is bright and represents one of the frontier developments at the point where education and gerontology intersect.

For current empirical support of the above statement, let us note the following and similar daily happenings that are "blowing in the wind":

1. The national survey of educational opportunities for the elderly in post secondary institutions conducted by the Academy for Educational Development and published under the title of *Never Too Old To Learn*, 1975.

2. The national survey of educational programs for the elderly conducted by Roger De Crow for the Adult Education Association of the United States of America, published under the title of *New Learning for Older Americans— An Overview of National Effort*, 1975. Now out of print.

3. Publication of the Adult Education Association of the United States of America, entitled *Learning for Aging*, edited by J. Grabowski and R. Mason, 1974. Now out of print.

4. The First National Extension Workshop on Aging held in Dallas, Texas, September 27—30, 1976.

5. The First National Congress on Educational Gerontology held at Virginia Beach, Virginia, June 7–9, 1976.

6. The First National Workshop on Aging and the Community School held in Flint, Michigan, October 6–7, 1976 under the cosponsorship of the Mott Foundation and the Administration on Aging.

7. The launching of the *International Quarterly of Educational Gerontology*, the first number of which appeared in the winter of 1976.

8. The rapid growth of the Association for Gerontology in Higher Education since its founding in May, 1972.

Our glorious land to-day
'Neath Education's sway,
Soars upward still.
Its halls of learning fair,
Whose bounties all may share,
Behold them everywhere,
On vale and hill.

Samuel Francis Smith
America

(Discarded stanza)

13

WILL SENIOR POWER BECOME A REALITY?

GEORGE L. MADDOX

Introduction

We bother to ask the question posed in the title of this chapter because the social and political visibility of older persons in the United States has increased markedly in this century. The social visibility of older persons reflects widely publicized demographic trends and the concomitant actual or anticipated strains on existing institutional arrangements for income maintenance, health care, transportation, and housing. The proportion of persons 65 years of age or older in our population has more than doubled since 1900 and is now about 10%. About one-third of the approximately 22 million older persons in the United States is very old, that is, 75 years of age or older. And the old and very old continue to increase at a higher rate than other age categories. For those who survived to age 65, the average future lifetime in years at the beginning of this decade was 13.0 for males and 16.6 for females. The social visibility of older persons has increased their political visibility. The older voter constitutes about 19% of the electorate and is as likely to vote as adults generally, and more likely to vote than younger adults. The political potential of older voters, if mobilized and selectively directed, is therefore consequential.

The prospect of a lengthened human lifespan, a debatable but not a fanciful proposition, could, in conjunction with a zero population growth, produce a population with a still larger proportion of older persons than at present. Even under conditions of zero population growth alone, we might expect older persons to constitute 16% of the population within 50 years. Although long-range population forecasting is necessarily tentative, depending as it does to an important degree on the future birth rates, an increasing proportion of older persons does now seem highly probable.

Careful observers of our institutional arrangements have increasingly expressed concern about the difficulty of providing adequately for income maintenance, healthcare, transportation, housing, and social services for elderly persons. The simple fact is that retirement and age-related disabilities insure a high level of demand on social resources. For example, persons 65 and older utilize health resources at a rate three times higher than adults generally. In the United States, a new healthcare industry, the nursing home, has been generated in the private sector primarily to serve disabled older persons. This industry has generated over 16,000 facilities and 1,175,000 beds and produces 369 million resident days of care. The average cost of this care is $479 per person per month and over $8 billion annually.

In 1973 the nation's total social welfare expenditures of over $215 billion rose 17% from 1960 and constituted 55% of all government expenditures. Obviously, older persons are not the sole cause for the rise in health and welfare expenditures; in any case, many have made and many continue to make substantial direct contributions to social insurance programs such as Old Age Survivors, Disability Insurance, and Medicare. Actually, current utilization of health and welfare services by older persons underestimates their needs. The 1971 White House Conference on Aging, for instance, documented in great detail the currently unmet social welfare needs of older persons. These developments are hardly reassuring to anyone already concerned about the current level of expenditures and the political implications of failure to meet the legitimate needs of a large number of voters.

Public discussion of social security legislation and national health insurance will inevitably focus attention on the special problems of older persons and remind us that political considerations are necessarily involved in determining what constitutes equitable distributions of social resources. The elderly and their social, health, and welfare needs are currently objects of such discussion for political decision making. Are the elderly themselves also active participants in these discussions and decisions which affect them directly? More precisely, is there a rising level of political consciousness among elderly persons which is producing, or may produce, a self-conscious politics of age in the decades ahead? In spite of the fact that there is increased societal awareness that older persons utilize health and welfare resources at a very high rate, failure to provide these services to a rapidly growing proportion of older persons could have, as one of its probable outcomes, a heightened political consciousness among older voters.

Interest in a Politics of Age

Interest in a politics of age among political and social scientists appeared belatedly in the 1950s. At the time the issue did not appear to be particularly urgent because the quiescent Townsend Movement, a political force in the 1930s, was the most visible evidence of a politics of age in previous decades. From the vantage point of the 1950s, chronological age did not appear to be a salient variable in explaining or predicting political behavior or a politics of age.

A White House Conference on Aging in 1961 focused national attention on the continuing problem of income maintenance in late life and on inadequacies of the health-care system. Legislative remedies were suggested. By the middle of that decade, Medicare and the Older Americans Act indicated that a politics of age could not be totally discounted. However, political activity tended to be in behalf of the elderly rather than by the elderly in their own behalf. Moreover, concern about the political attitudes and behavior of newly enfranchised youth diverted attention from the older voter in the late 1960s. Political observers who had been watching elders for a decade might have told the youth watchers a thing or two about the non-salience of age for political behavior. In any case, a politics of youth did not materialize. Nevertheless, political and social scientists have continued to exhibit an interest in aging and politics, if articles in professional journals are an indication. Dozens of articles exploring age as a variable in explaining political attitudes and behavior have appeared in the last decade. These articles have increasingly directed attention to identifying and solving methodological problems, which will permit discussions of aging and politics to move from informed speculation to definitive conclusions. As a result, we know a great deal about age, aging, and political behavior but not as much as we need to know. What we do know is summarized below.

Aging and Politics: A Balanced View

Colleagues at the Duke University Center for the Study of Aging and Human Development have systematically reviewed available evidence on aging and politics over the past four decades and have reached the following conclusions: First, interpretations of available evidence continue to be seriously compromised by faulty research methodology which confounds age, cohort, and time of measurement. Second, there are plausible competing explanations for any observed relationships between aging and politics. Political attitudes and behavior may represent the cumulative effect of the maturational process—the aging of voters. For instance, the hypothesis that conservatism is a concomitant of aging has a long history. However, the political behavior of those who are currently old may reflect particular experiences during the time of their political socialization, experiences of war and depression, so that generational or cohort experience rather than maturation may explain their behavior. We cannot discount the possibility that particularly significant events of a given period which affect all members of a population in a more or less similar fashion override both maturational and cohort effects. Our best evidence is that period effects appear to be very important in influencing political behavior and attitudes, generational effects less so, and maturational effects least of all.

Conclusions about age in explaining and predicting attitudes and behavior continue to be tentative rather than definitive, and contradictory findings are common. We find no evidence for an emerging politics of age. In fact, we believe that the global question: "Does age predict or explain political attitudes and behavior?" is probably the wrong question. We argue that a more useful question is: "Under what circumstances does age explain or predict political attitudes and behavior toward what issues by what older persons?" We have no reason to expect a simple answer to this complex question. In general, however, we have found that contemporary political events and generation or age cohort are more important than age alone in explaining political behavior, and that the further removed an issue is perceived to be from an older individual (e.g., national versus local issues) the less age explains his or her political response.

Published research has been preoccupied with four general questions regarding how aging is associated with (1) political interest, (2) political attitudes, (3) party affiliations, and (4) voting behavior. In regard to political interest and attitudes we know that older persons are as likely as younger ones to express continuing interest in politics and that older persons exhibit a wide range of attitudes toward a variety of political issues. Stereotypic identification of a politically conservative attitude with aging is an appealing generalization which has not been convincingly demonstrated. Clearly, cohort difference and societal trends in political ideology appear to be more important factors than age in accounting for observed distribution of voters in a conservative–liberal continuum.

A related issue is affiliation with a political party, a factor known to be related to voting behavior. Older persons are as likely as younger ones to report party affiliation. Moreover, as noted previously, older people vote with about the frequency of adults generally and more frequently than younger adults. This behavioral fact is better explained by two age-related characteristics—stability of residence and length of party identification—than by chronological age.

The actual and potential political involvement of older persons in the United States, we conclude, has been adequately demonstrated. The tendency to convert this involvement and potential into a politics of age in which elderly persons mobilize themselves in pursuit of special interests has not been demonstrated; quite the contrary. A sustained political movement among older persons frankly pursuing presumed self-interest has not been observed in the past four decades, but what about the future?

Age, Aging, and Political Behavior in the Future

Age and aging have not proved to be the most important factors in explaining political attitudes and behavior in recent times. We do not expect this to change in the next several decades and we reason as follows: In our society, age is one of the social characteristics which is used in allocating social resources. However, it is not the only social characteristic used in this way or, we believe, the most important one. Social status as indexed by education, occupation, and income is, for example, a better predictor than age differences in political attitudes and behavior. Social status also directs our attention to family groups, which are age-heterogeneous, intergenerational social units. One might expect, and limited research supports the expectations, that older persons do not ignore the claims on scarce resources made by younger persons; when generational claims are in conflict, both younger and older persons tend to emphasize the claims of younger persons. In the proceedings of the 1971 White House Conference on Aging, for instance, there were no hints or suggestions by younger or older delegates that more resources should be directed to the old at the expense of the young or vice versa. Instead, both younger and older delegates apparently wanted more social resources at the expense of what they labeled "the military establishment."

Political conflict between generations is, of course, potentially present and occasionally surfaces, as it did in an article by D. J. Stewart, entitled "Disenfranchise the Old" (1970). Such expressions, however, are the exception, not the rule. The failure of youthful voters to emerge as a potent political bloc in the late 1960s and early 1970s reinforces our argument that age per se is not characteristic of political behavior in this country.

Will this conclusion hold for the foreseeable future? Probably it will, although this prediction must be qualified by the following observations:

First, consider the locale of political behavior. Political issues are debated and decided variously at the national, state, and community level. Our generalizations about the non-salience of age for political behavior certainly apply at the national level and probably apply at the state and local level in the absence of contrary evidence. Although we are not aware of indications that a politics of age has been decisive or sustained in state politics or has even appeared as more than an isolated instance, local politics is the most likely place to look for evidence of a politics of age. We do not find a definitive test of sustained age polarization in local politics, but high concentrations of older persons are found in some countries and cities. In particular countries the proportion of older voters is in excess of 25%. Age polarization on, say, school bond issues could be consequential; but definitive evidence that age polarization occurs with frequency is lacking.

Second, the future political role of national organizations which ostensibly represent the interests of older persons remains problematic. Of special interest are a number of membership organizations for older persons which have attracted many adherents during recent decades. Prominent among them are the National Council of Senior Citizens, which has recruited several million members from the ranks of organized labor; the American Association of Retired Persons/National Retired Teachers Association, claiming more than six million members; and the National Association of Retired Federal Employees, with an estimated 150,000 members. The exact proportion of older persons who are members of one or another organization is now known but is obviously substantial. All the illustrated organizations engage in political consciousness-raising and in political activity on an ad hoc basis. Their effectiveness in the advocacy of national and state legislation in behalf of the aging and the aged and their potential effectiveness is untested and for the most part unstudied. To date they have not made frank attempts to mobilize their members as a self-conscious political bloc in pursuit of self-interest, and there are no indications of plans to do so. These organizations will be watched with interest since they now command considerable financial resources in addition to dues paid by members, they have developed effective organizational bureaucracies, they have members with experience in political participation, and they currently operate in a climate which encourages "interest group" politics. Organizations of older persons provide the structure for mobilizing a politics of age but do not in themselves predict such a development. These organizations may be effective in focusing attention on the needs of their constituents and in lobbying for appropriate legislative remedies by directing attention to their potential political power without having their bluff called. Such a strategy can be particularly powerful in a society whose prevailing ideology accepts increasing provision of health and welfare services as a desirable goal.

In Conclusion

Our reading of the evidence, then, is that in the absence of unforeseen increases in the proportion of older persons and a concomitant breakdown in the capacity of health and welfare institutions to deliver essential services, "senior power" in the sense of a politics of age and a self-serving gerontocracy is not the wave of the future. Moreover, problems of income maintenance, health care, and social services, although of special importance to older persons, are, after all, societal problems whose solutions affect persons of all ages. Whereas one might argue that an equitable distribution of resources would provide a larger proportion of our national wealth to the old, increased social security benefits and Medicare/Medicaid programs which provide tolerable services appear to undercut the emergence of health and welfare issues which could be used to mobilize older persons as a potent political force. In the unlikely event that a significant redistribution of national resources favoring the old at the expense of the young should occur, a politics of age might occur in which the young rather than the old could be the principal protagonists.

The possibility and probability of a politics of age at the turn of the century is realistically low; and so, it follows, is a gerontocracy.

Suggested Reading

Binstock, R. H. Interest group liberalism and the politics of aging. *The Gerontologist*, 1972, *12* (3), 265–280.

Binstock, R. H. Aging and the future of American politics. *The Annals of the American Academy of Political and Social Science*, 1974, *415*, 199–212.

Campbell, A. Politics through the life cycle. *The Gerontologist*, 1971, *11*(2), 112–117.

Cutler, N., & Bengston, V. Age and political alienation: Maturation, generation, and period effects. *The Annals of the American Academy of Political and Social Science*, 1974, *415*, 176–186.

Donahue, W., & Tibbetts, C. (Eds.). *The Politics of Age*. Ann Arbor: University of Michigan Press, 1962.

Douglass, E., Cleveland, W., & Maddox, G. Political attitudes, age and aging: A cohort analysis of archival data. *Journal of Gerontology*, 1974, *29*(6), 666–675.

Foner, A. The polity. In M. W. Riley, M. Johnson, & A. Foner (Eds.), *Aging and Society, Vol. III: A Sociology of Age Stratification*. New York: Russell Sage Foundation, 1972, 115–159.

Glenn, N. Aging and conservatism. *The Annals of the American Academy of Political and Social Science*, 1974, *415*, 176–186.

Glenn, N., & Zody, R. Cohort analysis with National Survey data. *The Gerontologist*, 1970, *10*(3), 233–240.

Holtzman, A. Analysis of old age politics in the U.S. *Journal of Gerontology*, 1954, *9*, 56–66.

Marmor, T. R. *The Politics of Medicare*. Chicago: Aldine Atherton, 1973.

Palmore, E., & Manton, K. Ageism compared to racism and sexism. *Journal of Gerontology*, 1973, *28*(3), 363–369.

Pinner, F., Jacobs, P., & Selznick, P. *Old Age and Political Behavior: A Case Study*. Berkeley: University of California Press, 1959.

Pratt, H. J. Old age associations in national politics. *The Annals of the American Academy of Political and Social Science*, 1974, *415*, 106–119.

Ragan, P. K., & Dowdy, J. J. The emerging political consciousness of the aged: A generational interpretation. *Journal of Social Issues*, 1974, *50*(3), 137–158.

Siegel, J. S. Demographic aspects of aging and the older population in the U.S. *Current Population Reports Special Studies*, May, 1976, Series P-23, No. 59.

Siegel, J. S., & O'Leary, W. E. Some demographic aspects of aging in the United States. *Current Population Reports Special Studies*, February, 1973, Series P-23, No. 43, p. 3ff(a).

Skolnik, A. M., & Dales, S. R. Social welfare expenditures, 1972–73. *Social Security Bulletin*, 1974, *37*(1), 3–18.

Stewart, D. J. Disenfranchise the old. *New Republic*, August 22, 1970.

Toward a National Policy on Aging. Washington, D.C.: United States Government Printing Office, 1973. Volume I and Volume II.

United States Vital and Health Statistics. Selected operating and financial characteristics of nursing homes. *U.S. National Nursing Homes Survey*, December 1975, Series 13: 22.

The Washington Post, August 13, 1970, p. A19.

14

A GERONTOLOGIST'S OVERVIEW

JAMES BIRREN

The chapters in this volume attempt to look at the future of aging and the aged from various viewpoints: social science, biology, and education. We see a reasonably optimistic picture that leads us to expect a somewhat better and longer life as the 21st century begins. This collective point of view might be called *cautious realism*, since beneath the surface of these commentaries are uncertainties about how older adults will fare in the next century. Some, who fear growing old, see in the growth of our older population a bleak future for the economy and perhaps even a decline in our civilization as a supposed gerontocracy arises. Although serious research, study, and discussions on gerontology are relatively recent phenomena, mankind has always been philosophically reflective about age and that closely correlated issue, death itself. Thus, the probability of dying is related to aging, and reciprocally, discussions on aging are often implicitly linked with thoughts of death or immortality. There is in much of our thinking about aging the influence of older ideas about aging and death which survive even in scientific patterns of thought.

The History of Aging and Death

Gruman (1966), in his excellent history of ideas about length of life and aging, points out that the current era is marked by a notable decline of confidence in religious beliefs which involve divine intervention to delay death. Our society approaches aging and death with less emphasis on religious thought and demonic influence than did our ancestors. Yet, while it is more open to ideas from the research laboratory, there is resistance and a counterwave in contemporary society. The reemergence of orthodoxy in religious belief might again encourage individuals to stress the importance of their relationship with divine powers rather than with scientific thought and research.

In forecasting the future of aging, various thoughts express the varying desires of a society to sponsor research on aging, to utilize results of that research in the design of society, and to provide services to aging individuals. A fundamentalist theological society might maintain that such effort is inappropriate, compared with the maintenance of a close relationship with the divine, in the belief that lengthening or improving the later years is undesirable. Another possibility is that the application of science or scientific experimentation might produce a holocaust which would weaken the hold of science and rationality on the value systems of technological societies. Use of the atomic bomb and the unleashing of technological power in declared and guerilla warfare has the potential for undermining the confidence of people in thought and science and strengthening the role of emotion in governing conduct. However, the fact that most people share a belief in science and its potential for "curing anything" also represents an emotional position. Nevertheless, it seems unlikely that the trend seen among some youth of today in embracing emotionally based creeds will supplant the rational and empirical traditions of our society. To the present author, this trend is probably the reflection of a subportion of the youth population that has been denied a strong identification. These youths are looking with hope and desire for a transcendent identification to give them the security, hope, and reason for being not found in their contemporary daily lives.

Many beliefs about aging and death are similar to the positions of conquered peoples who worship new gods while maintaining partial worship of the old. For example, there are several ancient legends about aging which still persist in modern times. Gruman (1966) has called these the *antediluvian*, the *hyperborean*, and the *fountain* types.

The first of these themes, the antediluvian, states essentially that ages ago people lived much longer than they do now. This belief is a version of the fall from paradise view that we were more perfect in the past, lived longer, healthier and happier, but fell from this state by our own shortcomings. Much of our folklore suggests that persons in the past who were close to God lived long and well.

The hyperborean theme states that somewhere in the world there is a group of people who live to be very old.

This is, perhaps, a version of the antediluvian theme, but it differs in that there is confidence that somewhere in the world there still exists that glorious state of paradise from which most people have been removed. In earlier years of civilization, communication with remote areas was difficult, and this gave the possibility for the confidence that there was indeed a people in a remote part of the world who possessed the secret of living a very long time. Even today we find a mystique about researchers investigating regions of the world where there are reported to be very long-lived people. There is a valid research strategy in studying people who have lifespans much longer than average. However, the press, which is in touch with what people want to believe, gives a cast to these reports which leads people to expect that quests be made to far off lands to find secrets not generally known and unobservable close to home.

The ancient waters or *fountain* theme persists into the present by belief in healing waters. The strength of this idea is shown by the many spas that exist in many parts of the world. Rejuvenation or cures of illness by bathing in unusual or miraculous waters are still being promoted.

To the preceding should be added the still current superstitious beliefs in charms and bracelets. And, while the current emphasis on improved diet is desirable, it, too, has an emotionally based mystique about it. Again, beneath the surface of the preoccupation with nutrition lies a conviction that by properly compounding a diet of mysterious, hard-to-get foods of rare purity the body will be more disease-free and endure much longer. The border zone of the irrational and rational in nutrition is difficult to discern but discussions with a diet zealot leaves one with the thought that there is more involved than the science of nutrition.

Superstitions and quackery often induce older adults to invest millions in promoting their good health and longevity. More money is spent on amulets and nostrums than on research on aging, which suggests how large is the emotional component in approaching the subject of aging. It would no doubt be revealing if one surveyed the beliefs of scientists doing research on aging. One might find a worship of both the new gods and the old.

Nineteenth century optimism held that there was an inevitable progress in human existence toward superiority. Educated persons believed that with study and thought progress would be inevitable. Benjamin Franklin, who lived in the 18th century, anticipated the general optimism of the next century with his belief in the inevitable advances of science. He even regretted that he was born so soon that he would not see or enjoy them. His thoughts about aging, too, were advanced for his day and were marked by the conviction that discovery of the causes of aging was close at hand.

The earlier part of the 20th century continued the extension of 19th century optimism. However, after World War II a counter theme of pessimism developed with existentialism as its sophisticated expression. Many became suspicious about science, government, and the institutions of society as the existentialists proclaimed there was no inherent meaning in the situation of man, and that he was but an absurd character playing out scenes in a meaningless drama. In contrast to the young, the aged are inclined to reject such views of life, for it is not easy to look back and say it had no meaning.

These streams of thought pervading our society provide the implicit substrate for the cautious realism of the
papers in this volume. These writers believe that progress is
possible in the conditions of growing old; but it will not be
an automatic outcome of inevitable progress, nor is it expected to be plucked from a single lucky discovery such as
the eating of the royal jelly that enables queen bees to
outlive their workers by many lifespans.

Concerns of Middle Age and Old Age

One of the common concerns of individuals is how long
they will live. A quotation from Gruman (1966) of Shryock
is pertinent here: "Condorcet, Franklin, and other 18th
century savants envisaged the indefinite prolongation of
life as a goal of science; but it has often been pointed out
that recent achievements have not extended the maximum
(and presumably biologic) limits of the lifespan. If the day
ever comes when a much higher expectancy is attained,
the most momentous results would obviously follow. The
future of society would then turn in no small degree on
developments in medicine, much as the outcome in
medicine has always depended in part upon trends in society." The early enthusiasts for the inevitability of scientific
progress have not been rewarded by any dramatic extension of the human lifespan. There are, however, some
reasons to be optimistic about small advances by the 21st
century. More likely than dramatic extensions of the lifespan at the upper end is the prospect that control over
stress diseases in middle age will add to our life expec-

tancy. This indeed will favor males since the male of today is more likely to succumb to the pattern of stress diseases, particularly vascular disease.

America does not have the longest lived population in the world. Certainly, by the 21st century Americans, with effort, might have a life expectancy equal to that in long-lived countries; in which case we might add about four years to the life expectancy at birth of men and about one year to the life expectancy of women. One of the puzzling features about the change in life expectancy is that it has increased more in females than in males as the conditions of life have generally improved. This exacerbates some of the social conditions of aging since men are usually older than women at the time of marriage and live shorter lives. It means, therefore, that the average woman has a considerable period of widowhood to face.

With the increase of the tendency to develop vascular disease because of stress and stressful social conditions, perhaps the health spa will reemerge with middle-aged and older adults becoming more interested in health. They may save money now being spent on quackery and instead go to centers where they are given information about diet, exercise, relaxation, styles of adaptation to stress, and the optimum management of chronic disease. In the context of forecasting, it seems that the health center of the future will no doubt capitalize on some of the motivational patterns of the past, but it will provide a more rational approach tied to research to improve individual and collective prospects for longer life. This, of course, adopts a realistic optimism that informed action can improve our well-being. Past approaches to medicine, however, have concentrated very much on the cure of disease.

The physician's training is primarily oriented to the detection and treatment of disease, rather than to the maintenance of health which requires a broader knowledge than the study of disease. The point should be made that health is too important a thing to leave exclusively to the physician who, by training, is primarily disease oriented.

Closely related to the question: "How long will I live?" is the question: "How healthy will I be as I grow older?" The chances are that the population will be healthier in the next century. Yet here again one finds optimistic and pessimistic counter themes. For example, Gruenberg (1976) points out that the introduction of antibiotics brought with it a greater improvement in life expectancy for the less fit. In particular, it was noted that in the preantibiotic period mentally retarded persons often died early from influenza and pneumonia. Use of antibiotics now results in such retarded persons surviving into their seventies, suggesting that as more individuals live longer in the middle years there will collect, in the older population, increasing numbers of individuals who have multiple disabilities. This view holds that the older population will degrade rather than improve as more people survive. As yet, we do not have sufficient data to judge whether the health in the older population is improving or declining; but it should be noted that from life expectancy data it appears that life expectancy after age 65 has improved, though not as much as life expectancy at birth. If the population is degrading, life expectancy at age 65 should indeed be lower than it used to be; but such is not the case. Admittedly, however, life expectancy does not itself tell us about the health and disability of the population.

Quality of Life

Older individuals are often said to be more interested in the quality of life rather than in the quantity of it. Certainly a life void of quality is hardly worth extending. It is generally thought to be reflected in such matters as housing, income, and privacy. One can expect improvements in all of these by the 21st century. Older adults today are finding more congenial housing and higher retirement incomes than in the past. The key issue seems to be an adequate income with which the older individual might pursue better housing and other material comforts in the market place.

While the concept of retirement communities has often been criticized by the younger observer, whether professional or nonprofessional, retirement nevertheless is a feature of our society. An age-integrated society does not actually exist since people cluster by age because of similar interests and needs. The retirement community has not emerged as a segregated community with overtones of a ghetto for the aged. It has provided at least one clear model of choice, a choice that many individuals have made. If the recent past is a clue, one will see more development of these specialized communities to serve older persons.

It always comes as a surprise to younger people that many older adults experience life's high satisfactions. There is a myth that the over-65 join ranks of poor old folks whose satisfaction level is so low that life is unbearable. The findings of social science research report that life satisfaction is not unduly low in the aged; and many older adults report greater satisfaction at their present late stage of living than do young adults. The evidence suggests that most older adults have not grown old, sick, poor, and lonely. Indeed, they are more concerned with opportunities for learning and experimenting with life than the young are prepared to believe. This supports the view that we are breaking down the past concept of aging as a single thing surrounded by many bad consequences. It is bad to grow old and to be sick, poor, and lonely; but there has been a change in view that growing old, of itself, is not bad.

Increasingly, in America, there will emerge a positive model of growing old. It will probably begin with the increasing awareness of older persons who "have it together," those who might be called the elite or accomplished aged. These are the people whom life refines and polishes. They move toward greater mastery of events and their adaptive strategies are such that they are increasingly strong and confident with the passage of years. There are still those, however, who become more handicapped with the years and drop further toward the bottom of society. If there are drop-outs in the young perhaps one should speak of the fall-outs in the aged—those people who acquire multiple disabilities of health, behavior, and life circumstances. There is, in immunology, the concept of an immunizing level of exposure to a foreign agent in contrast to a sensitizing or infecting level. The drop-out aged have been overpowered and have not developed immunity to the many facets of living, as opposed to the accomplished aged who behaviorally, socially, and physiologically have developed immunity and are perhaps stronger as a result of the longer years.

Given the fact that the chapters of this volume show that the aged will be better educated and certainly more informed, we may anticipate that our institutions of higher learning will be increasingly turning to the many needs of mature adults in society. It can be expected that in the 21st century every institution of higher learning will have research programs at the biological, behavioral, and social levels on the issues of aging and have substantial material in the curriculum on adult life and aging.

At present, the late adolescent, who is not yet into the major roles of society, and the older adult are more alienated than the middle-aged who are preoccupied with the running of society and the management of their large responsibilities. Given a population of accomplished aged who are informed and are information seeking, it is likely that there will be increasing speculation about the meaning of life in a broad and philosophic sense. In response to this, one may see a resurgence of the humanities, including philosophy, which recently have been considered irrelevant to the education of the young in a technologically oriented society. Through the humanities there may be a renaissance in helping the mature adult achieve an integrated approach to life and in providing concepts and opportunities for deriving meaning from existence. No doubt biologic and related research on aging will also be enhanced. In brief, I am forecasting a graying of the university in which individuals of all ages will be seeking knowledge about the conditions of life, and an informed and eager population will be interested in extending its options in life and, with maturity, in contemplating its meaning.

References

Gruman, G. J. Transections of the American Philosophical Society. Vol. 56, Part 9, Philadelphia, 1966.
Gruenberg, E. M. The Failure of Success. The Rema Lapouse Lecture, American Public Health Association, October, 1976.

Index